What people are saying about

Reality Squared

Reality Squared faces down reality TV with the curiosity and seriousness that the subject deserves and so rarely receives. In Syverson's hands, there are no lazy cliches or easy jokes — he cuts to the heart of why and how this form carries political and cultural consequence. From *Vanderpump Rules* to the reality presidency we're all forced to watch, Syverson provides a necessary theoretical framework to help us understand a phenomenon that isn't going anywhere anytime soon.
Lucas Mann, author of *Captive Audience: On Love and Reality TV*

Elegantly written, Tom Syverson's *Reality Squared* is at once a love letter to reality TV and a nuanced study of one of the most pervasive forms of media in our contemporary moment. Amid debates on how leftist discourse has been making excessive use of bad faith and paranoid readings, Syverson discursively intervenes with a generosity that does not disavow a rigorous, critical assessment.
Kristen Cochrane, @ripannanicolesmith

Reality Squared proposes a novel idea that's achingly overdue: rather than wringing our hands over the obviously staged aspects of reality television, perhaps it's better to think of these mechanisms as a perfect map of our increasingly fictitious world. Syverson's dead-on understanding of cheap entertainment and its symbiotic relationship to the failures of the Left make this an invaluable read.
Jarett Kobek, author of *Only Americans Burn in Hell* and *I Hate the Internet*

Syverson forces us to contemplate and wrestle with the possibility that reality television represents not so much a "staged" version of our lived existence, but rather a mirror for our own fictively structured social universe. At a time when it so often feels that the truth has become stranger than fiction, Syverson's dive into the world of reality television suggests a more uncomfortable "truth": there is no longer a meaningful difference between the two.

Naomi Snider, author of *Why Does Patriarchy Persist?*

In a so-called post-truth era, underwritten by the interminable logic of finance, and with a former gameshow host and professional wrestling guest star as president, Syverson invites readers to take seriously that reality television might be the paramount artform of our time. Far from obfuscating reality, its precise performativity plays back the implausibility, instability, and irrationality of our own lives in extraordinarily legible ways. Playing reality shows like *The Hills*, *The Real Housewives*, and *The Bachelor* against ideas from cultural theory, psychoanalysis, and critical theory, Syverson argues that reality television serves as a kind of ethical matrix and, perhaps, a way station onto a grander political consciousness. It is hard to agree with every argument, claim, or provocation but, just like its source material, it's hard to turn away either. *Reality Squared* plays precisely in a murky zone where one considers what happens if we really do stop being polite and start getting real.

Ajay Singh Chaudhary, Brooklyn Institute for Social Research

Reality Squared

On Reality TV and Left Politics

Reality Squared

On Reality TV and Left Politics

Tom Syverson

Winchester, UK
Washington, USA

JOHN HUNT PUBLISHING

First published by Zero Books, 2021
Zero Books is an imprint of John Hunt Publishing Ltd., No. 3 East St., Alresford,
Hampshire SO24 9EE, UK
office@jhpbooks.com
www.johnhuntpublishing.com
www.zero-books.net

For distributor details and how to order please visit the 'Ordering' section on our website.

Text copyright: Tom Syverson 2020

ISBN: 978 1 78904 581 9
978 1 78904 582 6 (ebook)
Library of Congress Control Number: 2020933329

A CIP catalogue record for this book is available from the British Library.

Design: Stuart Davies

UK: Printed and bound by CPI Group (UK) Ltd, Croydon, CR0 4YY
Printed in North America by CPI GPS partners

We operate a distinctive and ethical publishing philosophy in
all areas of our business, from our global network of authors to
production and worldwide distribution.

Contents

I'm not a housewife, but I am real.
Bethenny Frankel

Chapter 1

Don't Believe Anything You Don't See on TV

One way we came to terms with Donald Trump's election to the United States presidency was to tell ourselves it wasn't real.

To be more specific: it was real, but it wasn't *quite* real. The latter half of November 2016 saw millions of people suddenly knocked off kilter, stumbling and weeping as they awoke to find themselves dreaming. The dream—in the sense of an abstract vision—was always a familiar metaphor in our political imagination. But this time, center-liberalism was elbow-deep in nightmare. Famously, Otto von Bismarck described politics as the art of the possible; after Trump, it'd involve supervising the impossible. The next few years of political life would be a terrorizing mix of fantasy and reality, never quite conforming to the dictates of either pole. In this way, Trump's election was not only a shocking political development, but also a decisive moment in redrawing the metes and bounds of social reality. As novelist Jarett Kobek put it:

> Donald J. Trump, the world's best approximation of living fiction, whose body appears to be constituted of media coverage stitched together with plastic surgery, was elected to the Presidency of the United States of America...Reality collapsed into fiction.[1]

For the political mainstream, the problems posed by Donald Trump were sui generis. He wasn't just another crooked politician or fattened racist. He was something much more disorienting. From the beginning, Trump's entry into politics was the wrong kind of pop-culture incursion. He married tabloid celebrity with electoral politics so successfully that it forced a new legitimation crisis for democratic capitalism. After all, for democracy to have any sense, mustn't the political sphere separate itself, at least to some modest extent, from the trashy habits of mass culture? But Trump represented all at once the many ways the polis could be defiled, whether by commerce or counter-meritocracy, giving body to an unspoken fear among elites: that democracy always had, within it, the potential to go too far.

What were supposed to be his failings—a compulsive ability to enrage and titillate audiences; a stained persona of lowbrow consumer artifice; and a singular reputation for crass, cruel, and duplicitous behavior—these were in fact his greatest powers. With warmed-over Reaganism and overtures to the ugliest social resentments, his campaign tied together in one vulgar display all the darkest manipulations of commercial advertising theory. As it turned out, baffling audiences with bullshit was no liability, but rather an unlikely gift. The key was to understand how flimsy the laws of social reality always were; that even the unwritten rules of public knowledge were meant to be broken.

It was in this context, amid an ostensible breakdown of reason in a society gone mad with frivolity, that a purveyor of lies qua entertainment had become president. Who, or what, was to be blamed?

Some said reality television.[2]

Trump's actual career in reality television dovetailed nicely with that explanation. He'd been the icon of NBC's *The Apprentice* and *Celebrity Apprentice* all through the Bush and Obama years, and he'd made several memorable appearances on pro wrestling, that masculinist older brother to reality television.[3] As far as his public image went, there was never a clear demarcation between fabricated and fake personas, nor a line between his entertainment endeavors and political ambitions. "Life is not all sincerity," he's supposed to have said. "Life is an act, to a large extent."

As such, his knack for carrying out an insidious, lifelong form of method acting preceded him, and only a month after his election, this dual persona—epitomizing the lowest form of celebrity and holding the highest political office on the planet—followed him directly into the White House.

In December 2016, *Time* ran a piece by Jeff Nesbit, former communications director to Dan Quayle, titled "Donald Trump Is the First True Reality TV President." The president elect had by then confirmed that he'd maintain an ownership stake in NBC's *Celebrity Apprentice*, and though he would no longer host the show, he would hang onto an executive producer role. But truthfully, maintaining this pecuniary thread to reality television was only a metaphor for a much broader characterization of his presidency as something terribly unreal. In *Time*, Nesbit offered up a paradigmatic diagnosis:

> [The Trump presidency] will look and feel a lot like a political reality TV show played out on a grand stage, with producers scripting the biggest fights behind the scenes while leaving plenty of room for unrehearsed, populist public drama. Trump is the first truly made-for-television president. Every day will literally be a new episode shot in real-time, in front of a public and a world that simply can't get enough of the spectacle.[4]

A year into his presidency, Trump had already embraced this characterization himself.[5] He greeted reporters by saying "welcome back to the studio." In press conferences, he boasted of high ratings and great reviews.

Was this anything new, or had hysterical liberal commentators suddenly lost their perspective? After all, how fabricated was George W. Bush's salt-of-the-earth drawl, or Bill Clinton's charade of moral rectitude? In many ways, conceiving of politics as socially useful improvisational theater was old hat. For decades before Trump, politicized for-profit media like cable news and talk radio had already been dominant in shaping public perception, particularly on the right. Likewise, pseudo-news programs like *The Daily Show* helped craft mass liberal identity, which formed along a chain of condescending jokes punctuated by rhetorical orgasm. Particularly as the entertainment industry continued to hold itself out as somehow political, only the most naïve among us could be scandalized by the thought of politics as entertainment.

Be that as it may, the gravity of an ascendant Donald Trump collapsed everything fake or frivolous about politics into an over-potent node, now radiating lies directly from the White House. For many, Trump was the logical conclusion of our terrifying, shameful, and now deadly conflation of fantasy with reality. But how, and in what way, was this narrative useful? For one thing, it served the intelligentsia as it struggled to reconcile the conditions of Hillary Clinton's loss with its own unflagging sense of superiority. If the story were true, then Hillary never lost on the merits after all; her only mistake was in failing to realize she was on a game show. Next time, all that had to be done was to change the channel, from E! back to C-SPAN.

Or so we thought.

* * *

A few months into the Trump administration, the picture would complicate itself significantly, and its implications for political culture would resist easy interpretation. Before we knew it, the moment took on a strange vocabulary of pop epistemology. Paradoxical concepts like "fake news" and "alternative facts" became common in political conversation as the line between fact and fiction grew blurrier and blurrier. Sean Spicer conjured an imaginary audience to declare the president's inauguration to be the most well-attended in history. Kellyanne Conway repeatedly referred to a fictional event called the Bowling Green Massacre to justify the administration's travel restrictions. The central political question of the early Trump era wasn't a choice between competing policy programs—or traditional dividing lines like race, class, gender, or foreign policy—but rather whether the very notion of truth had any shared meaning at all anymore. It was a subject until then confined to philosophical salons and Philip K. Dick novels; but now it was being discussed openly on CNN and at White House press briefings.

The year we elected Trump, Oxford Dictionaries chose "post-truth" as its word of the year. It was defined as "relating to or denoting circumstances in which objective facts are less influential in shaping public opinion than appeals to emotion and personal belief." The adjective had increased in usage by 2000 percent that year.[6]

The uncanny pseudo-reality emanating from the Trump administration took on a darker and more complex tone when viewed alongside the theoretical tenor of his most insidious supporters. A brief examination of the eccentric theoretical foundations of the alt-right (and alt-light), now understood to be a new and dangerous force in America, reveals a political culture in the midst of a reckoning with social reality itself.

What was the ideological context of such an alarming development? Angela Nagle has argued, controversially but persuasively, that by the time Trump took office the Right had come to be characterized by everything the Left used to be: "The libertinism, individualism, bourgeois bohemianism, postmodernism, irony, and ultimately the nihilism that the left was once accused of by the right actually characterized the movement."[7] This included adopting a playful and sometimes outright hostile relationship to truth, "where every statement is wrapped in layers of faux-irony, playfulness and multiple cultural nods and references." For Nagle, this transgressive right-wing postmodernism was the natural enemy of left-wing

5

class materialism.[8]

Once considered the key failing of a degenerate left academia, the Right's shift away from observable reality and toward the chaos of cultural meaning meant that Trump was no garden-variety liar. Instead, he embodied the negative truth of the lie, and he was its natural tactician. Thus, the situation we faced was not a straightforward contest between liars and truth-tellers, but rather a far more expansive and disturbing shift in cultural metaphysics. Viewed in this light, the first reality television president was also the first postmodern president.[9]

What's postmodern? Though it remains a term subject to repetitive academic litigation and clarification,[10] for our purposes we can define postmodernism loosely as the idea that reality and truth consist in whatever those in power assert to be real and true. It can be thought of most basically as a theoretical orientation critical of whatever is taken as *given* in mainstream discourse, shaped as it is by unseen powers and unconscious ideologies. Already, many liberals today prefer to associate the notion of ideologically mediated reality with right-wing quackery, but traditionally postmodernism has been a creature of far-left thought. Generally, and again imprecisely, we might point to the French post-structuralism of Baudrillard, Foucault, Derrida, and Lacan; gender deconstructionists like Butler, Cixous, and Irigaray; and the critique of Enlightenment rationality and culture industry by the Western Marxists of the Frankfurt School.

But now, those playing with the relationship between power and discourse were right-wingers.[11] Perhaps the apotheosis of this strange overlap came in August 2018, when Rudy Giuliani declared on *Meet the Press* that "truth isn't truth." A meme followed, superimposing an image of Giuliani on the cover of Jean-François Lyotard's seminal work, *The Postmodern Condition: A Report on Knowledge*.

This unusual convergence of right-wing agitation with left-wing epistemology did not go unnoticed on the Left. A piece in *Jacobin* argued that if the far Right had adopted a postmodern critique of reason, then it was the duty of socialists to return to rationalist Enlightenment values.[12] The piece suggested not only that postmodernism was an ineffective analytic framework for today's politics, but that the split was fundamental: "The alt-right will always outflank the postmodern left because, in the words of Mike Pence, the former are 'coming home' while the latter are attempting to camp on alien territory." In other words, as Jürgen Habermas has argued for decades, socialism is rational and scientific by its very nature, while fascism is characterized by superstition, mysticism, and an innate distrust of social facts.

Either way, a theoretical turn had occurred by which the dialectical musings of the Frankfurt School and the lofty French theory of the former century had come to resemble too closely the reactionary psychosis of the present one. Seizing the ostensible moment, reasonably worded materialist outlets like *Jacobin* and *Current Affairs* emerged to offer a pitch for a new, lightly scientific brand of socialism.

Across these publications and others, a new wave of materialist-left explanations for Trump began to gain currency as a result: the death spiral of identity politics and deteriorating race relations in the superficial Obama years; the implosion of the Republican party as a manageable political institution; the hollow embrace of progressive neoliberalism by the Democratic Party; and most of all the story of capitalism, class, and crisis since the late 1970s. For a new generation of socialist activists, most notably those within the swelling ranks of a resurgent Democratic Socialists of America (DSA), these explanations were compelling, and they laid the theoretical foundation for countless activist actions, reading groups, and primary challenges.

But it has always been possible that this debate between culture and economics—repeating that old duel between base and superstructure—now provides an outmoded and misleading framework for coming to terms with Donald Trump's ascendancy. Indeed, as Fredric Jameson has argued, postmodernism consists in precisely the eclipse of a distinction between the two, such that "the cultural and the economic thereby collapse back into one another and say the same thing." As a result, it remains unclear whether orthodox left materialism still serves as a viable mode of political analysis, let alone something that can generate a workable ideological basis for a movement capable of competing with the populist right.

Indeed, outside of DSA reading groups and sporadic Twitter threads, mass political culture remains preoccupied on both sides with either vulgar theodicies or flagrant conspiracy theories, and one can hardly conceive of a mainstream American politics anymore that is not structured by the every tweet and blunder of Donald Trump himself. While academics were pontificating about the political legacy of Heidegger and Derrida, and while leftists renewed old debates about base and superstructure, the most salient explanation on everyone's mind was simpler: in a society constituted by mass-media experiences and virtual interactions, a fraud like Trump was the inevitable result. More specifically, the conflation of facts and fantasy via reality television laid the foundation for the degradation of public discourse and the disruption of social reality.

Like it or not, the political culture we face today remains mired in a thoroughly postmodern jumble, and untangling it will take new forms of thinking, and in particular a renewed understanding of what it feels like to be a person today.

* * *

It's not the primary object of this humble book to undertake a comprehensive explanation for the problem of postmodernism or the relevance of class-first politics. Many of the Left's finest thinkers, including a number of those with whom I tend to agree, would question the wisdom of analyzing political problems without a firm anchor in materialism and class analysis; and yet, as Lenin once noted, an intelligent idealism is still superior to an ignorant materialism. To the extent that material analysis still serves as the basis for left politics, it'll need to be an intelligent materialism that thoughtfully takes into account the complexities of mass media, has the ability to navigate our increasingly fragmented social reality, understands the dominant role of aesthetics in the cognitive-cultural economy, and doesn't shrink from the pervasive strain of doubt and distrust running throughout our political institutions, voting behaviors, and bases of material power. In other words, there's a contingency that the Left must begin to prepare itself for: What do we do if it turns out that we can't put the genie back in the bottle?

Insofar as this book does have a primary object, it will seek to provide a theoretical account of reality television and the conditions of its significance today. In order to begin doing so, a few more words are necessary, as a means of laying introductory context, on the relationship between reality television and political life. At the very least, it remains incumbent on me to begin to justify how anybody with the slightest concern for progressive politics, or any form of political morality for that matter, could justify watching reality television after Trump — let alone writing a book about it.

In short, if the befogging of fact and fiction has been a boon to the Right, then what does that mean for the Left?

In his classic formulation, Lyotard defined postmodernism as an "incredulity towards metanarratives." For Lyotard, a metanarrative was a shared understanding to justify knowledge in some way beyond its bare utility. The postmodern condition does not so much entail disposing of the notion of observable, structured reality, but rather draws our attention to our shared inability, or unwillingness, to agree on which stories to tell about it.

Within the frame of postmodern politics, the efficacy of a resurgent scientific socialism now embraced by contemporary democratic socialists—a linear emphasis on material conditions and concrete conflicts—is perhaps less of a panacea than some of us want it to be. But while it's too early to tell, we might consider that an effective materialist politics might require its own postmodern turn. In our rush to oppose Trump, we risk forgetting our own lessons and casting off too much of the Left's own critical tradition. In so doing, we lose sight of the social complexities we remain subject to, with or without Trump. As one writer argued in *The Outline*:

> Isn't it disheartening — how quick we are to sacrifice postmodernism at the altar of politics? Solipsistic thinking is a real danger, especially in the hands of a far-right government...But at its best, postmodernism offers something essential: a key to mapping the complex terrain on which the many falsehoods of the Trump era are manufactured.[13]

For example, the facts of wage stagnation are crucial, but they do not obtain significance by reference to an epistemological distinction between liars and truth-tellers. Rather, the facts of inequality are useful to the Left only insofar as they are embedded in a plausible political narrative. To imagine politics as a site of struggle between scenes that are staged and those that are faithfully depicted is to misapprehend the real conflicts at stake. The social disorientation of our current moment suggests that our most immediate political struggles won't be epistemic or metaphysical in nature, but rather material and ideological, and thus decidable only as a matter of political willpower. Power is not a question of adjudicating claims to truth; in fact, as Humpty Dumpty famously argued in *Through the Looking Glass*, the resolution of competing truth claims is precisely the opposite: "The question is which [of us] is to be master—that's all."

The Right understands this well, and it goes a long way toward explaining its dominance in this moment. For instance, as David Harvey has argued, the ideological hegemony of neoliberalism today doesn't result from its triumph in the marshaling of economic facts, but rather from the mobilization of class power and the social instantiation of an intelligible metanarrative of market fundamentalism. Crucially, neoliberalism has been a successful project of "theoretical utopianism," but it has been a total failure as a technical matter.[14]

Similarly, the political economists of the Austrian school, in forming the theoretical foundations of neoliberalism, didn't view themselves as bland technicians, but rather saw themselves as intensely moralistic thinkers. The underpinnings of their thought can be traced to the reactionary cultural philosophy of Friedrich Nietzsche, in particular his reverence for the individualistic elite and concomitant disdain for the mediocre multitudes.[15] Crucial to both Nietzschean aesthetics and Austrian economics is the structural necessity of social hierarchy in preserving the very concept of value. Thus, as one peels back the layers of rhetoric gleaned from Economics 101 classes, beneath the right-wing's concrete economic program is just more metanarrative.

In the neoliberal metanarrative, the story of market politics is a progression toward greater and greater freedom for all. You can stamp your feet and point to Thomas Piketty's data all you like—and don't get me wrong, you should—but in a postmodern moment such as ours that won't be sufficient without first rediscovering a metanarrative of socialism, equality, and the promise of a humane future. Like the fantasies of market fundamentalism that do so much work on behalf of the bourgeoisie, a socialist metanarrative need not be experimentally demonstrable to be politically effective. Any fan of reality television will tell you: it doesn't matter what's staged and what's not. The program need only be compelling.[16]

In this simple sense, reality television helps expose the

false dichotomy between privileged facts and mere fictions. Understanding reality television isn't simply a matter of negotiating a conflict between fact and fiction; rather, the genre is about generating their synthesis. The decision incumbent on the Left is not whether facts exist or whether we can measure them; rather, it's a question of how to marshal and interpret those facts, how to conduct our story editing and produce an engaging show for voters. Which facts we point to depends on what we want to build with them. It's precisely within the context of a postmodern blurring of fact and fantasy that we can open up a dialectical space of meaning, taking control of both the facts we encounter and the stories we wish to tell about them.

Through the lens of reality television, this book considers the extent to which we can confront today's postmodern condition by accepting it on its own terms. Fredric Jameson's touchstone work on postmodernism famously considered "the enormity of a situation in which we seem increasingly incapable of fashioning representations of our own current experience."[17] For Jameson, the postmodern "death of the subject" also meant the death of authentic style and expression, resulting in a situation in which "aesthetic production today has become integrated into commodity production generally." Pushing beyond Jameson's classic observations, this book argues that reality television is the postmodern art form par excellence, and as such the only mode of expression capable of properly aestheticizing life in a world in which artistic representation itself seems to be failing us.

In reproducing the process of fictively structured reality, the phenomenology of reality television approximates the postmodern experience, which is a human condition as mediated by virtual formations. Joan Didion famously said that stories are how we render life bearable in the first place; today, the most acute examples of this palliative function of storytelling occur on reality television.

Importantly, this book is not about how we or anybody else can defeat Trump, the resurgent far Right, or global finance capitalism. In fact, we might as well just proceed from the assumption that watching reality television is as shallow a consumerist act as any other, and that in many ways writing this book is no more political an act than tweeting about *Harry Potter*. But in what follows, I hope to establish that there is nonetheless an essential difference forming between the two types of entertainment—*Star Wars* on the one hand, and *Real Housewives* on the other—insofar as the former provides a childish escape that tells us nothing about how life is really lived today, while the latter provides a more exciting and useful gateway to understanding. At its best, reality television shows how postmodern life is constructed and, more importantly, how it feels for us to take part in it.

A fortiori, this book also stands to refute the notion that reality television is illegitimate or undignified because it manufactures a sense of reality, rather than communicating something preexisting about it. Primarily through the work of Jean Baudrillard, Fredric Jameson, Slavoj Žižek, Jacques Lacan, and Jodi Dean, we'll see that this commonplace view has all but lost its consistency.

Understanding reality television requires first accepting the premise that reality is by no means an external given, but rather a condition of social relation.[18] To the extent that it's a useful concept at all, "reality" does not refer to much on its own, and it should never be understood as existing outside of our apprehension. Rather, reality is produced through a shared, intersubjective process of symbolization and communication. Reality comes together as an interplay of shared understanding, a virtual edifice built by signifiers, which are parcels of relational meaning with an agency all their own. We do not speak through signifiers; rather, as Lacan famously claimed, it's the signifiers that speak through us.

As in reality television, signifiers are the "producers" of linguistic reality, manipulating us from the outside and installing us into an external symbolic framework. The purpose of being placed within the symbolic order is to be dolled up and presented for the gaze of another. This structure of meaning, upon which we all rely for subjective consistency and access to social reality, forms according to an autonomous logic that generates narrative to hold itself together. To claim that reality television is "staged" is simply to restate the process of social reality's formation in the first place; reality television is the same process carried out at another level of abstraction.

Fredric Jameson once described dialectical thinking as "thought to the second power, a thought about thinking itself, in which the mind must deal with its own thought process just as much as with the material it works on."[19] This book's working definition of reality television follows from Jameson's model of dialectics. Reality television is reality squared; it's a form of representing social reality that says something about social reality itself.[20]

The formal structure and aesthetics of reality television reflect back at us all the most dynamic characteristics of subjectivity today. To name a few: We exist continuously in the gaze of a Big Other, unseen but apprehended. Our contingent experiences are punctuated by internal confessionals and regulated by retroactive attempts at narrative. Our behavior is driven by a destructive thirst for drama and a recognition that, in a Schumpeterian sense, crisis is what generates the most potent lived experiences. In reality television we recognize the simulative labor of our own psychic processes.

Contrary to many liberal critiques of so-called post-truth politics, our ability to construct and narrativize social reality need not be a dangerous anarchy. Rather, it can be a wellspring of human creativity and progress. Likewise, reality television can be both an object of critical analysis and a worthy avenue of narrative pleasure. The reason for this apologia is not in spite of, but precisely because of, the bizarre cultural metaphysics we face in today's postmodern political moment. In a social context so fundamentally ambivalent about the relationship between data and narrative, we're caught between the cold-hard facts and the stories we need to tell about them. But studying reality television reveals the choice between fact and fiction to be a false dilemma. Reality television emerges not as a dangerous site of epistemic contamination, but rather as a useful and thoroughly contemporary vehicle for exploring the fictive truths of human experience.

That is, if you're willing to give it a chance.

Chapter 2

When People Stop Being Polite and Start Getting Hyperreal

In Michel Houellebecq's novel *The Map and The Territory*, a photographer achieves fame by taking pictures of maps. The maps represent the territories, and his photographs represent the maps. Later, the photographer works with an author who plans to write about the photos, adding a third link in the chain of abstraction. Readers encounter yet another level when they learn that the writer in the story is named Michel Houellebecq.

The purpose of the novel's focus on cascading representation is revealed when Houellebecq—the fictional Houellebecq—is savagely murdered. Houellebecq stages the death of his fictional double, a gesture of authorial suicide, to demonstrate the impossibility of fixing a lodestar of meaning in any one spot. Once caught in the circuit of meaning, we find ourselves lost in the *mise en abyme* of multiple abstraction, like two mirrors facing each other. The signifying chain goes all the way down, only to loop up again. There is no bottom to meaning and no final guarantor of any one signifier's place in the symbolic order.

Houellebecq's novel takes its title from Jean Baudrillard's *Simulacra and Simulation*, one of the classic texts of postmodern thought. In it, Baudrillard argues that postmodern society is characterized by a conflation of reality with representations of reality: "it is a question of substituting signs of the real for the real."[21] This conflation forms a state of lived simulation called hyperreality. In this state of affairs, "it is no longer a question of either maps or territories. Something has disappeared: the sovereign difference, between one and the other."

To show what he means, Baudrillard starts by considering two types of feigned illness. A person can fake being sick, for instance, by complaining of nonexistent stomach pains, or by introducing a croak into one's voice and surrounding oneself with crumpled tissues. In this way, one can pretend as if an actor in a play; the outward fabrication masks an ascertainable underlying reality.

But what about the more difficult case of someone with Munchausen syndrome or hysterical conversion disorder, whereby symptoms are not merely performed by the complainant, but actually suffered? Here, the person isn't acting in any traditional sense, and the underlying reality of her health is no longer so easily ascertainable. This scenario presents a more disorienting question because it demonstrates the difference between pretense and simulation. As Baudrillard clarifies, "simulating is not pretending...pretending, or dissimulating, leaves the principle of reality intact: the difference is always clear, it is simply masked, whereas simulation threatens the difference between the true and the false, the real and the imaginary." Today, the integrity of medicine and diagnostic psychiatry depends on its ability to distinguish between real and simulated disorders, and "it is against this lack of distinction that classical reason armed itself in all its categories." In other words, rationalism and empiricism were well-equipped to handle pretense, but simulation was harder to grab onto and tame. By the late twentieth century, Baudrillard argued, the difference between the two was becoming increasingly obscured.

Writing at the tail end of the 1970s, Baudrillard offered a number of then-contemporary examples to illustrate the ways in which social and political experience had come to resemble a simulated hyperreality rather than a traditional, authentic reality: Disneyland as simulated culture, the Cold War as simulated conflict, and Watergate as simulated political scandal. In each case, society broadly acts as though it were faced with the real thing, but behind each of these mass representations there lies no concrete referent. There is no American idyll reflected in the microcosm of Disneyland; the principle of mutually-assured destruction rendered nuclear war the one event sure never to happen; and the trivial hijinks of Watergate were child's play when viewed objectively within the cruel machinery of global capitalism. And yet, these simulacra, these images with no referent in reality, were the animating themes of the late 1970s and early 1980s, inescapable and irreducible to mere lies.

Importantly, Baudrillard wasn't proposing more conspiracy theory. Simulation has no particular agency, and it's not a matter of these things being a hoax. Rather, the fact of their simulated nature is ascertainable by virtue of openly known and admitted facts; simulacral on its face, acknowledging the madness of our uncanny unreality does nothing to remove it from the center of our concern.

Since *Simulation and Simulacra* was published, neoliberalism and the financial crisis have only made the concrete brutalities and inefficiencies of global capitalism more apparent. But concomitantly, our political narratives have grown ever more hyperreal. Under George W. Bush, the dreamwork of neoconservativism and its perverse fantasy of militarily installed utopia led to the loosely defined War on Terror, as well as a chain of disastrous attempts at regime change. The War on Terror has been a simulated war par excellence: amorphous, voluntary, objectless, and circular in producing its own cause. Obama's presidency had the uncanny effect of performing progress in race relations even as those same relations deteriorated to new lows. His administration's global drone strikes and campaigns of domestic surveillance are facts that continue to resist integration into the popular consciousness. No matter how often the Obama administration's sins are repeated or how thoroughly they're documented, they are simply overwhelmed by Obama's simulacral celebrity, a hyperreal construct that exists independently of any concrete deed.

In the Trump era, Americans now may choose between two

equally hyperreal scenarios: either Russia controls American democracy from behind the curtain, or Donald Trump is a highly sophisticated political tactician. Those are your options. Any understanding of our political situation not keyed to either of these hyperreal scenarios is foreclosed from the public imagination. Caught between a lie and a falsehood, American political culture is held together by the all-encompassing histrionics of social media, the irrationality of which is directly proportional to its influence. Baudrillard himself could hardly have concocted so thoroughly hyperreal a world as the one we live in today.

* * *

But perhaps no example of the hyperreal is more striking than that of reality television. Like the slippage between pretend illness and simulated illness, the scope of reality television culture has broadened to the point that we can no longer distinguish between the real events filmed and their televised depictions. Even if we succumb to the crude commonplace of referring to it as substantially "staged" content, in attempting to render reality television as mere pretense we erase the border between actor and role. Consider Baudrillard's example of a staged bank robbery. To the extent that you can achieve a successful simulation, "the network of artificial signs will become inextricably mixed up with real elements." As a result, you will be arrested and tried like any real criminal. At a certain level of sophistication, sincere attempts at illusion morph into the real.

After all, if reality television is peopled by shrewd actors, is it not strange that these hidden thespians should be so secretive of their skill? Isn't movie acting still more lucrative? And at what point does a successful subject of reality television begin acting? As Trump himself has shown, to be a successful reality television actor is to undertake a lifelong method-acting campaign, not only as the show progresses from season to season, but even before the camera starts rolling. If your staged personality is going to "read" on screen, you must get a substantial head start. One must design and build up the performative plausibility of one's simulated persona long before filming begins, indeed before one is selected for participation in production. It's an acting class that stretches back in time to the first words and steps of an infant predestined for celebrity.

Ultimately, a real person in a fabricated scenario *lives* that scenario, and as that life is lived onscreen, we're left with the uncomfortable inability to distinguish between the real life and its televised representation. One might begin to wonder whether this person's real life, as distinct from the conditions of its representation on screen, ever happened at all. Such an aporia is the essence of hyperreality.

Baudrillard proposes four phases of the image as we proceed from reality to hyperreality. We can easily adapt them to reality television:

- Reality television is a faithful depiction of its subject's authentic life;
- Reality television is a fake depiction of its subject's authentic life;
- Reality television hides the fact that its subject no longer possesses an authentic life;
- Reality television faithfully depicts the authentic life of no real subject.

Baudrillard's point here is not to privilege any particular level of the framework. Rather, for Baudrillard, these phases of understanding are "all simultaneously true. It is the secret of a discourse that is no longer simply ambiguous, as political discourses can be, but that conveys...the impossibility of a determined discursive position." In other words, the experience of hyperreality entails our very inability to sort one level of representation from the other. If only it were that simple, we could simply unmask the truth and be on our way. But, for Baudrillard as much as for sincere devotees of reality television, it's never, ever that simple. We can't simply elect to disavow the condition of hyperreality, either as a means to interpret the actuality of reality television or to escape the perilous political context explored in the previous chapter.

"Imposter phenomenon" was a term coined by psychologists in the late 1970s, right when Baudrillard first began writing about hyperreality. It referred to an extreme lack of confidence prevalent among professional women, characterized by "an experience of feeling incompetent and having deceived others about one's abilities."[22] Originally, psychologists thought that this was explicable by gender, but it turned out that both men and women suffered imposter feelings in roughly the same proportions.

Today, imposter syndrome affects roughly 70 percent of people across multiple demographics.[23] That means that a large majority of people today feel as though they were actors playing a role rather than living real lives. Imposterism is often associated with career, but it can more broadly apply to any gap between our self-image and the way we believe we're perceived by others. For example, with respect to measuring our own intelligence, we have two options: either I am an intellectual fraud that must pretend to be smart in order to impress others, or I am overwhelmingly intelligent compared to others and must downplay my intellect so as not to alienate them. No matter the objective conditions of one's life, those experiencing imposterism are moved to interpret themselves in a way that renders their outward appearance fictitious. So even at an individual level, we are marred by a disconnect between what we are compelled to designate as reality and the reality that we experience personally.

But imposterism is not mere self-deception, nor is it a garden-variety case of low self-esteem. More than a simple neurosis, the hyperreal turn occurs when one considers the fact that social science has demonstrated beyond a doubt that factors fully unrelated to one's objective ability—such as race, gender, sexual orientation, socioeconomic background, etc.—have an appreciable impact on one's prospects for success in life. If 70 percent of people feel like imposters, it stands to reason that many of them are precisely that: imposters, frauds, and simply the beneficiaries of unfair social biases or dumb luck. Our desire to be fair to ourselves and avoid cultivating a toxic self-image is at odds with what we already know about how society works. We'd like very much to trust in the authenticity of our lives, but such confidence is elusive.

* * *

The commonplace of imposterism is but a hint of a greater deformation in Western subjectivity that has been experienced over the last 50 years or so. Fredric Jameson has argued that the dissolution of traditional subjectivity has been a key characteristic of postmodernism, under which the "creative" subject's historical condition of anxiety and alienation is replaced by depthlessness, polyvocality, and fragmentation.[24] Whereas the modern subject was whole, contained, and atomized, the postmodern subject is instead "decentered": mobile and scattered along a chain of different contexts and subject positions.

The singular, bourgeois subject turns out to be a historically specific construction of capitalism's initial stages, an article of faith that late capitalism has been busy eroding and transforming, for its own purposes, for decades. Culturally, we're faced then with the disintegration of the singular point of consciousness from which the great works of modernism emanated; postmodernism instead constitutes the field in which each of us moves but cannot be fully located, as one form of what Jameson called "the Heisenberg principle of postmodernism." Anticipating his subsequent work on postmodernism, Jameson had in the early 1970s observed in *Marxism and Form*,

> The former subject no longer thinks, he "is thought," and his conscious experience, which used to correspond to the concept of *reason* in middle-class philosophy, becomes little more than a matter of registering signals from zones outside itself... The subject wrongly continues to assume that there exists some correspondence between inner monadic experience and that purely external network of circumstances (economic, historical, social) which determines and manipulates it through mechanisms beyond the horizon of individual experience.[25]

In more or less typical Marxian fashion, those determinant mechanisms beyond the individual's grasp and awareness consist mainly in the peculiar economic base of late capitalism, with the fragmented subject emerging as a response and adaptation to its invasive, colonizing dynamics:

> Now, when the entire business system...depends for its very existence on the automatic sale of products which no longer correspond to any kind of biological or indeed social need... marketing psychology obliges [capitalism] to complete its conquest of the world by reaching down into the last private zones of individual life, in order to awaken the artificial needs around which the system revolves.

In other words, capitalism's never-ending need to generate greater and greater consumer demand results in an odd fictionalization of economic reality, whereby the proper subject of postmodern capitalism must necessarily be placed at a remove from concrete reality, and distanced as well from its own sense of unity and continuity. The tools of mass consumerism are indispensable to forming this condition:

> Advertising, market research, psychological testing, and a host of other sophisticated techniques of mystification now complete a thorough *planification* of the public, and encourage the illusion of a life-style while disguising the disappearance of subjectivity and private life in the old sense.

The result is a subject that is "no longer able to distinguish between external suggestion and internal desire, is incapable of drawing a line between the private and the institutionalized, and finds itself therefore wholly delivered over to objective manipulation." Where, indeed, is the line between one's integral subject and consumer culture? How much of what used to be called the soul or essence of humanity is now a stabilizing mirage of mass consumerism? These are the most interesting questions of subjectivity that were already apparent in the early 1970s, at the dawn of late capitalism and before any of us had seen anything yet.

Today, consider simply the multiplicity of voices, identities, and faces that we put on every day in the context of modern communications technology. At any given moment of an ordinary day, I might be carrying on a half-dozen remote conversations at the same time. These interactions take place over a number of digital platforms—iMessage, G-chat, Twitter, Facebook, Slack—and within each platform, overlapping social permutations form subsets of threads and groupings. Each context requires its own highly specific set of relations and unspoken social expectations, such that I'm a particular "me" in each varying context. I have one voice on Twitter and quite another one when texting my mother, and yet these communicative operations can be carried out seamlessly from minute to minute. Today, from the palm of my hand, it's not simply "code switching" that occurs from app to app, but also shifts in my identifiable personality. Across an index of group texts, conversations that are appropriate among one combination of recipients could be inappropriate if just one person were added or subtracted from the mix. In fact, I might carry on simultaneous conversations involving the same exact person across two different platforms or threads, with the tone and content of our communication differing substantially in each simultaneous context.

This is to say that digital communication has amplified the spectral and polyvalent nature of human personality, rendering our identities themselves hyperreal; quite apart from there being any "real me" buried beneath the social media profiles, group chats, and other forms of instantaneous remote communication, I am instead something fragmented and decentered, occurring *across* these different forms of outward appearance and modes of sociality.

It is for this reason that it makes so little sense to speculate whether reality television stars are "acting" or showing their "real selves." That hypothesized real person can never be located in any concrete sense because it doesn't exist. At best, a celebrity's hidden authenticity can be defined only as the inverse of everything we *do* know about them, whether from episodes, recaps, rumors, or gossip rags, and thus becomes a structural concept rather than one defined by epistemic validity. That hidden self may even be the most tenuous and put-on part, compared to the vitality and permanence of their public-facing persona.

The prospect of indulging in the hyperreal can be exciting and liberating for this reason. Remarkably, Baudrillard already had reality television in mind when he was writing *Simulacra and Simulation*. In 1971, the vérité television experiment *An American Family* provided the prototype for contemporary reality television, following the everyday lives of an ostensibly typical

American family. Upon seeing it, Margaret Mead immediately recognized it as the storytelling vehicle of the future, "as new and significant as the invention of the drama or the novel—a new way in which people can learn to look at life, by seeing the real life of others interpreted by the camera."[26]

In a striking passage, Baudrillard outlined an "aesthetics of the hyperreal" that in one stroke distills the hypnotic pleasures of reality television:

> It is not a question of secrecy or perversion, but of a sort of frisson of the real, or of an aesthetics of the hyperreal, a frisson of vertiginous and phony exactitude, a frisson of simultaneous distancing and magnification, of distortion of scale, of an excessive transparency. The pleasure of an excess of meaning, when the bar of signification falls below the usual waterline of meaning: the nonsignifier is exalted by the camera angle. There one sees what the real never was... Pleasure in the microscopic simulation that allows the real to pass into the hyperreal.[27]

In other words, the hyperreal aesthetics of reality television operate by transforming our relation to the real from a framework of banality into one of marvel. Reality television opens up a distance between viewer and subject by virtue of the camera's mediation, while at the same time bringing us much closer to a real person than we're ever normally permitted. In this process, everyday banalities are transposed to objects of sustained regard.

By and large, it's a mistake to assume that reality television is enjoyed by mediocre viewers and appreciated for its mediocrity. Rather, what is at work here is an aesthetic move similar to the one made in magical realist literature: The commonplace is rendered fantastical and the fantastical is rendered commonplace. As viewers, we become intimate with somebody as incomprehensibly famous as Kim Kardashian only by watching her eat salad while standing at her kitchen counter. The baubles of her unimaginable wealth fall away in the image of her whining and goofing off with her sisters. There's a certain measure of security that forms by virtue of our trust in the fact that whatever happens in front of the camera, it always already matters. In these ways, we get from reality television what is too often lacking in the real: meaning and enjoyment in life as a matter of course.

Chapter 3

Dance Like Someone Is Watching

The third episode of *American Crime Story: The People vs. O.J. Simpson* opens with Robert Kardashian taking his family out to lunch. When they arrive, the restaurant is packed. But the hostess recognizes him, and so the family is ushered in past the line. Though pleased with their sudden privilege, the Kardashian family soon realizes there is a price to pay for celebrity: As they dine, they're surrounded by gawking onlookers. Their lives have irrevocably entered the public eye. Social power in the form of celebrity entails a loss of anonymity, and striking such a bargain isn't always consensual.

In the midst of this epiphanic moment, a young Kim Kardashian notes that O.J. Simpson is literally her godfather. In doing so, the short scene extrapolates the incidental social links between O.J. Simpson and the Kardashian-Jenner family, suggesting a much broader homology between sensationalized news media and reality-based celebrity.

But before the FX series, celebrity chronicler Lili Anolik anticipated this connection.[28] Writing in *Vanity Fair* in 2014, Anolik argued that O.J. Simpson was the "baby daddy" of reality television, as the trial gave birth to the reality genre's first slate of stars. In addition to the subsequent careers in reality television proper that the trial produced—from Faye Resnick's notorious stint on *Real Housewives of Beverly Hills* to Kato Kaelin appearing on a handful of unremarkable competition shows—the O.J. trial also discovered the character of media spectacle itself. Anolik writes, "What made the Simpson case reality-TV-esque, too, was the awareness that it wasn't reality, that it was reality at one remove. So intense was the media scrutiny that...[trial participants] were both characters in the drama and observers standing outside the drama watching themselves be characters in the drama." Anolik notes too how the shift occurred by a sleight of programming; trial broadcasts literally interrupted and replaced regularly scheduled soap operas, trading one form of sensational drama for another.

Today, the figure who best channels the radical potential of reality television is no longer Kim Kardashian, but Donald Trump. Apart from the rumor that he intended to have O.J. Simpson appear on season two of *The Apprentice* (but for Simpson's 2008 armed-robbery incident), Trump is the person most acutely responsible for the subsuming of modern reality in the hyperreal, its reach pushing beyond the way station of mere entertainment and into the realm of statecraft.

In this connection, consider as well that Andy Cohen — Trump's political enemy and simultaneously a fellow impresario of reality television — got his start in newscasting. Cohen remarks, "I always loved news and I always loved entertainment, so I feel like I just kind of married the two...I use a lot of the skills that I learned at CBS News over those 10 years, [like] recognizing great characters."[29] Cohen may be a famous fan of soaps, but his formal training took place in the context of an evolutionary mutation of journalism, from a record of concrete facts to a floating, noncommittal imitation of such.

Indeed, another facet that the creators of the FX series sought to establish was the shared origins of reality television and the 24-hour news cycle. Trump himself is well-known to love cable news, with some commentators speculating that some of his presidential conduct is directly informed by whatever happens to be on Fox News that day.[30]

But to dismiss this as merely one more of Trump's buffoonish idiosyncrasies is to engage in a comforting reduction. The president might be in the grip of corporate media, but who, exactly, is not? Whether you watch Sean Hannity or trawl Twitter all day, it's difficult to dismiss the extent to which our social relationships and political identities are formed and regulated less and less by our concrete experiences, and more and more by the digital media we consume.

In many ways, any comment on the 24-hour news cycle is already outdated. A media experience confined to a few hours in front of the living-room television set is almost quaint, compared to the intravenous drip of information we now absorb online. Push notifications, RSS feeds, livestreams, and instantaneous social media interactions constitute mass media at its most assaultive. Today we are compelled, from within and without, to absorb and assimilate high-velocity information, the stream intensifying and accelerating each time a new phone or app comes out. To engage with the world at all is to stand up to this hammering barrage of data.

The informational assault of mass media was another thing Baudrillard forecast decades ago, and he associated it with a radical loss of meaning in the social space. "We live in a world where there is more and more information, and less and less meaning." These words could've been lifted from the latest handwringing column about social media, but Baudrillard wrote them more than a decade before Nicole Brown's murder and a quarter-century before the first iPhone. Already by the early 1980s, information was being delivered to people at levels that were becoming unmanageable. Since its inception, mass media has been, by design, overwhelming, disorienting, and inescapable. Baudrillard was moved to speculate that:

> information is directly destructive of meaning and signification, or that it neutralizes them. The loss of meaning is directly linked to the dissolving, dissuasive action of information, the media and the mass media...Where we think that information produces meaning, the opposite occurs. Information devours its own content. It devours communication and the social.

His argument suggests that information has become so abundant, and its delivery through mass media has become so multivocal, that the traditional poles of communication— sender and receiver—have collapsed upon each other. Now, the receiver selects which message it would like to receive in advance, in effect becoming its own sender. This entails a circularity that engenders the hyperreal: "Is it the media that induce fascination in the masses, or is it the masses who direct the media into spectacle?" It's unclear who holds the power in this "reabsorption of every dialectic of communication in a total circularity of the model," and Baudrillard doesn't even seem to think it's such a bad thing.

But for our purposes, what it does point toward is the importance of television in structuring social reality.

* * *

A fiction film provides a useful metaphor. Dan Gilroy's *Nightcrawler* (2014) tells the story of freelance video-journalist Louis Bloom (Jake Gyllenhaal) and his relationship with jaded TV executrix Nina Romina (Rene Russo). As a producer of televised news, Nina describes her professional ideal to be "a screaming woman running down the street with her throat slit." Lou is all too eager and capable of delivering on that order, as he crawls the nighttime underbelly for footage of sleaze, tragedy, and bloodshed.

Nina presents the classic stereotype of an amoral media mogul. She's a greedy manipulator who beams violence and tragedy into our homes for profit. But this cliché has a remainder in our own gaze: If the media is degenerate, is this not a reflection of our own degeneracy? Apropos of a hyperreal system, *Nightcrawler* cannot untangle whether our bloodlust is the result or cause of media-simulated reality. But where Baudrillard would read a radical collapse of meaning in this impasse, Lacanian psychoanalytic theory suggests how the news media is not a destroyer of social meaning, but rather its agent.

One thing that makes *Nightcrawler* unique is the unlikable nature of its protagonist. Viewers notice immediately that for a main character, Lou is somehow "off"; a certain cruelty undergirds his professional aspirations, forming a picture of the classic sociopath. Lou masquerades as normatively ambitious, assertive, and rational, but in fact he is missing an irreducible substance of human decency.

From the Lacanian perspective, this missing substance is a proper relationship to language. As Žižek explains in *How to Read Lacan*:

> The sociopath's use of language paradoxically matches the standard commonsense notion of language as a purely instrumental means of communication, as signs that transmit meanings. He uses language, he is not caught up in it, and he is insensitive to the performative dimension. This determines the sociopath's attitude toward morality. While he is able to discern the moral rules that regulate social interaction, and even act morally in so far as he establishes that it suits his purpose, he lacks the "gut feeling" of right and wrong, the notion that one just cannot do some things, regardless of the external social rules.[31]

In other words, Lou is a sociopath in the sense that he only sees language as a means to an end; normal people live inside and through our language, but Lou only uses it as a tool. The "true" Lou is not caught up in the circuits of linguistic meaning, but located somewhere else. Words appear to him like cold algebraic constructs, denotative but not connotative, rather than the "living" embodiments of human emotion, desire, spirit, and experience.

In this unusual relationship to language, a sociopath like Lou is estranged from what Lacanian psychoanalysis calls the symbolic order, otherwise known as the Big Other. The symbolic order is the external network of signs and signifying relationships that we must enter before we can communicate and socialize with others. It principally includes language, but it's broader than that too. The nature of the symbolic order is twofold: It's "big" in the sense that it's powerful and not subject to individual human control, and it's "other" in its location outside of us. We must go to it, and once there, follow its rules. The alternative is to fail to make sense on a social level, and thereby lose touch with others.

In short, the symbolic order as Big Other is the neutral matrix through which we can communicate and relate to one another. Direct communion, circumventing the Big Other's strictures, is strictly impossible. The human body forms in the womb, but human subjects are born only in language. As Žižek puts it, "to become operative, it is not enough for all concerned individuals to know some fact; 'it,' the symbolic institution, must also know/'register' this fact. This 'it,' of course, can ultimately be embodied in the gaze of the absolute 'Big Other,' God Himself."[32] Just as we constitute social reality via the Big Other as language, so too do we constitute it via the gripping omnipresence of what is called God. In both cases, our terrifying and meaningless subjective experience is harnessed and transformed using a neutral matrix, one that is in the first instance fundamentally alien to us. What is God? What is language? The answer is the same: "the agency for which one has to maintain [an] appearance."[33]

The nature of Lou's sociopathy is that he has one foot in and one foot out of the symbolic order. He can reach out and touch the Big Other, but he comes and goes as he pleases; it's his plaything, not the condition of his grip on social reality. This failure to fully internalize the outer symbolic network deprives him of the ability to give meaning to his actions or to see value in others.

But herein lies *Nightcrawler*'s crucial metaphor. Toward

the middle of the film, Lou is talking to Nina in her television studio. While touring the broadcasting floor, Lou is stunned by the studio's cardboard cityscape backdrop. In awe Lou declares, "It looks so real on TV." For Lou, things aren't quite real until they're on television; in other words, television is his Big Other. Elsewhere in the film, when we see Lou hovering over dead bodies with his camera, the film depicts the carnage with a cold distance. The primary experience of Lou's external world is not yet "reality" at all, but rather a kind of pre-reality that has yet to be fully integrated into the symbolic order. As mere sensory data, the sounds and images he observes lack meaning. But through filming, Lou integrates real events into his relationship to reality. For something to count as real—real in the social register, in the sense that he's capable of sharing it with others—Lou needs there to be a screen between him and the world outside.

For us, this is precisely the role of language: to act as the medium through which we can stabilize intersubjective relations and stay "on the same page" with each other. That is to say, our primary sensory experience and internal affects are only constituted as "reality" once situated within a certain representational frame, that is, within the virtual framework of language and other symbols. In an important sense, our experiences must pass through a certain process of fictionalization before they can become social reality.

Nightcrawler's formal technique nails the idea, employing a brilliant screen-within-a-screen motif. We watch Lou watch his own reality form through camera lens and cathode-ray tube. Some of the most striking and emotionally jarring scenes in the film involve not Lou's primary experience of violence and destruction, but rather the characters' secondary experience of re-watching that violence on television, on a screen-within-a-screen.

Nightcrawler's conceit is to flip the commonplace narrative of mass-media spectacle. Rather than a process of perverting social reality, mass media is what forms it as such. The raw footage, its bare sensory information, tells us nothing. Before it can function as a locus of meaning, it must be placed in the context of an evening news broadcast, edited, narrated by news anchors, and offered in a space of a social justification. The contingent moment must not only be captured, but retroactively transformed into a broadly intelligible symbolic gesture.

Nightcrawler demonstrates that only after the primary "real" experience has been in a sense fictionalized — structured by symbols and given narrative distance — can we begin to understand it. Our place in the world thus depends not on cold-hard facts, but rather on the far more human process of "wrapping our mind around" those facts. Such is the fictional basis of social reality.

* * *

Primetime news is only a metaphor. The necessity of virtual constructs — concepts, metaphors, references, customs, assumptions, clichés, all the many unstated expectations of human behavior — is a broad condition of social reality. The fields of reality and fantasy are not opposites and cannot be construed as separate registers; rather, it's through the process of symbolic-fictionalization that we pass from real to reality. Reality here is not the objective truth imagined by positivistic science, but rather the standards by which we define appropriate behavior, draw acceptable conclusions, and enter into social relationships with one another on a day-to-day basis.

This is so, not only on the scale of public spectacle, but also within the register of personal identity. The Big Other is the linguistic field by which we form and enter into social reality, but it's also the external means by which we shape our internal self. The symbolic interpenetrates our psyches and binds us to one another. This is how Žižek can analogize the role of the

Big Other to that of God: It's the gaze that falls upon us even when we're alone, guaranteeing the capacity of our actions to be interpreted as meaningful.

Žižek offers the metaphor of an analysand who has sex with her husband purely so that she can tell her psychoanalyst about it: "the analyst is here the big Other, the agency for which one has to maintain the appearance (of the ongoing sex life)." In other words, the significance and meaning of sex is not limited to biological imperatives or physical pleasure, but rather to the fact that we intuitively trust in the interpretative significance of sex; that, if someone else were to hear about it, it'd be something worth hearing about.

In constructing our personal identities, we don't rely on a literal outside observer to interpret our thoughts and behavior. Nobody out there comes to assure us that we're appropriately inscribed in the symbolic order. Rather, we unconsciously hypothesize a viewer. Contrary to the banality so often recited, to live out a human identity is to dance as if someone is watching — always watching.

The more accurate cliché is one cited by Hannah Arendt, which she borrowed from Cicero: we're never less alone than when we're by ourselves. Even in solitude, we understand that everything still counts because it's all unfolding in view of some omniscient gaze that ascribes meaning and significance to our actions. Otherwise, without an outside referent to swing from, our day-to-day struggles, our hopes, our joys — all of it would lose meaning. And that wouldn't be much of a real life at all. Without the notion of the Big Other, the universe is a disorganized swirl of random incidents, with no story and no sense. This isn't a religious claim, but rather a description of what it means to be personally situated in social reality.

The move from real to reality is about imposing semiotic structure on an otherwise empty, random string of events. The bargain we strike is to play along with its fictions and simulations;

in return, we receive meaning and social relation. A life worth living is one that can be raised to the level of a story. Recalling Joan Didion, we might say that life's central task is to produce its own narrative. To acquire such meaning requires the crutch of human culture in all its richness, historicity, and creativity.

In reality television, meaning requires recourse to the symbolic grammar of a lower order of abstraction: cinematography, film editing, story editing, music cues, after-the-fact narration, and episodization.[34] Although it seems paradoxical, in reality television cast members become themselves—become real—to the extent that they inhabit their simulated selves. In order to do so, cast members must provide the cameras and audience—here playing the role of Big Other—with the fullest performance possible. Žižek notes, "in the social-symbolic reality things ultimately *are* precisely what they *pretend* to be," meaning that in the gaze of the Big Other there's no distinction between your inner authenticity and the way you act on the outside.[35] Insofar as our inner subjectivities are constructed from external semiotic elements, including intersubjective recognition by others, there can be no such distinction between who one is on the outside and who one is on the inside; if anything, the latter corresponds to the real deception.

With Žižek's Lacanian framework in mind, we can resolve the apparent paradox of imposter syndrome mentioned in an earlier chapter. Recalling Žižek's classic formulation of ideology—as that which we enact by ironically disavowing—consider the following example. A recent law school graduate may not "feel like" a lawyer. But as far as the Big Other is concerned, the law graduate's feelings are irrelevant to the integrity of her social identity. By drafting legal memoranda, filing motions, appearing in court, i.e., by faking it in every way possible, precisely by becoming the imposter, she'll be recognized on the outside as a lawyer, and thus she emphatically *is* a lawyer. As Mark Fisher has noted, the same idea undergirds Christopher

Nolan's *Batman Begins*. There, it's a moral claim made explicit by the film's crucial line: "It's not who you are inside that counts, it's what you do that makes you who you are."[36]

Reality television provides the screen-within-a-screen that models this same relationship, standing in as the mediating filter between individual and symbolic order. In reality television, the camera plays precisely this role of the Big Other; here, producers and film crew form "the agency for which one has to maintain [an] appearance." The cameras do not themselves manufacture or inform a show's sense of consistency; rather, they allow and enable that reality to emerge in the sense of *becoming something that matters.*

* * *

Lastly, it's important to understand how symbolic fictions structure our personal relationships. Žižek points to the special status of the empty gesture in our everyday dealings with others.[37] For Žižek, the nature of the empty gesture is twofold: it's devoid of actionable content (i.e., it's never meant to be acted upon or taken literally), and yet at the same time its offer is socially obligatory.

Consider a situation in which a benevolent uncle bestows a gratuitous pecuniary gift upon his nephew, a recent high school graduate. How does the nephew properly accept such a gift? By rejecting it. The nephew says, "Oh no, I can't accept this. Please, you're too kind. You must take it back." The uncle, receiving these empty gestures of abnegation, now has the opportunity to reoffer the gift profusely, folding his arms and refusing to take the gift back. "No, no, I insist, please you must take it." Only now is the nephew free to accept the gift unconditionally: "Well, alright, if you insist!"

What is the point of this empty roundabout? As Žižek notes, "the point, the magic, of symbolic exchange, is that although in the end we are back where we were at the beginning, the overall result of the operation is not zero but a distinct gain for both parties, the pact of solidarity." Thus, not only do hollow motifs insinuate themselves in our real relations, but in fact these bouts of make-believe are what render those relations possible. And further, it's the specifically fictional nature of these gestures that allow them to work their magic.

To take an empty gesture as literal, and then to act upon it as though it were filled with positive content, would represent the most disorienting of social faux pas:

> The need for the phantasmic support of the public symbolic order (materialized in the so-called unwritten rules) thus bears witness to the system's vulnerability: the system is compelled to allow for possibilities of choices which must never actually take place, since their occurrence would cause the system to disintegrate.

In this sense, "Fantasy designates precisely this unwritten framework which tells us how we are to understand the letter of the law" and thus "structures our belonging to a community." Narrative is what ties us to the symbolic order in the first place: fantasy forms the basis of social reality. Similarly, Troy DeVolld argues that what's important in the production of reality television is not authenticity as such, but the fastidious appearance of authenticity. He refers to this as the central principle of reality television production: "The integrity and perceived authenticity of story cannot be compromised...The suspension of disbelief necessary for viewers to immerse and invest themselves in other types of TV shows still applies to reality."[38]

The empty gesture shows how fantasy constitutes community at the social level, but its role in the realm of romantic and sexual relationships is even more acute. The classic Lacanian dictum that "there is no such thing as a sexual relationship" is interpreted to hold that direct sexual relations are impossible without the mediating support of fantasy. As Žižek puts it, "any sexual pleasure that we find in touching *another* human being, is not something evident but inherently traumatic, and can be sustained only in so far as this other enters the subject's fantasy-frame."

In normative sexuality, the purpose of fantasy is to hold the other person close but at a safe distance. A relationship disintegrates not when it becomes subsumed by fantasy, but rather when that fantasy dries up. To cross a certain threshold of intimacy with someone can be traumatic and terrifying, causing us to panic and run in the other direction. The "Real" of another human being is, perhaps tragically, too much to bear. What may be attractive at one distance can become repugnant upon closer examination. The same can be said for the Lacanian distinction between the stability of reality as compared to the disorienting trauma of the Real:

> The gap that separates beauty from ugliness is thus the very gap that separates reality from the Real: what constitutes reality is the minimum of idealization the subject needs in order to be able to sustain the horror of the Real…Here we can see how fantasy is on the side of reality, how it sustains the subject's sense of reality: when the phantasmic frame disintegrates, the subject undergoes a loss of reality and starts to perceive reality as an "irreal" nightmarish universe with no firm ontological foundation; this nightmarish universe is not pure fantasy but, on the contrary, *that which remains of reality after reality is deprived of its support in fantasy.*

Reality television restages this imposition of fantasy on the Real of human relationships. Its production process functions analogously to fantasy as that which supports the reality of another person and saves us from their excessive proximity.

On reality television, the strongest friendships are those that have been "staged" or simulated for many years past their real expiration date. One can sustain such an excruciating pact of solidarity only within a thoroughly phantasmic space. For instance, had they never been on *Real Housewives of Orange County* together for so many years, would Vicki and Tamra still have anything to do with each other? Again and again, their friendship is destroyed and reborn from season to season, losing its consistency only to tread back upon safe phantasmic territory when the cameras begin rolling again.

Žižek suggests: "Perhaps the feature which characterizes true friendship is precisely a tactful knowledge of when to stop, not going beyond a certain threshold and 'telling everything' to a friend." Like sex and romance, intimate and lasting friendship is only possible if both parties are decked in the armor of fantasy, safe enough from the traumatic Real of the other person that they can continue to be close.

We see the same phenomenon played out in house-of-strangers shows like *The Real World* and *Jersey Shore*. Obviously, it's not the cast members' offscreen lives that provide the structure or substance of these touching and tumultuous friendships; rather, the shows' emotionality emerges from highly constructed scenarios—and this is precisely the source of their power. On these shows, friendships are born fully enveloped in the safe space of fantasy, as cultivated by the cameras and internal scenario. Dialectically, the structure of house-of-stranger situations fosters an excessive proximity, which is the source of so much calamitous drama; but the proximity is sustained by the virtual, insofar as it depends on the "staged" context of those relations to form and maintain their integrity. Put another way, the house-of-stranger scenario creates a formal structure of interpersonal distance that unlocks the housemates' intense emotional intimacy. Housemates can "tell everything" and "go there" with each other precisely because it's "only for the show." In service to the show's scenario, the ontological threat of otherwise traumatic intimacies is provisionally suspended; excessive intimacy is rendered safe. But without this phantasmic frame, no such intimacy would have the chance to take hold. People would simply not open up to each other, as we fail to do every day in the vast majority of our contacts with people in our day-to-day lives.

Take, as a final example, perhaps the most famous friendship in reality television history: Lauren Conrad and Heidi Montag. Such was the central conflict of *The Hills*: the establishment, deterioration, and irreparability of their friendship. Before getting wrapped up in the show's dramatic saga, one might question whether their friendship was ever real, or whether the girls interacted with each other, from the beginning, purely for purposes of filming. Did Spencer really drive a wedge between them, or was it all a cynically instigated producer ploy? These bland interpretative options merely return us to Baudrillard: The fact that it's produced with cameras, editing, music cues, and voiceover already means we cannot receive the show's content as unmediated Real—and nor should we. We already know that the friendship between Lauren and Heidi was premised largely on fantasy, but so are our own relationships in the real world. Like any great friendship or romance, the dreamlike medium in which the story unfolds is what solidifies its significance in the first place.

Lauren and Heidi's friendship bloomed in front of the camera, and this was also the way that audiences can understand and ascribe significance to their actions. The performative operations that Lauren and Heidi had to make in order to be friends with each other—allowing themselves to be seen by others, agreeing to have a particular conversation at a particular time, measuring and reformulating their speech into intelligible, assemblable lines of dialog—these are all compromises of the same sort that we make when we form our own "real" relationships with others. A certain level of performance is the precondition for our submission to social reality.

In essence, an effective reality show does not cover up the cast members' real feelings toward each other, nor does it try to fully invent them; rather, its conceit is to render intelligible to our collective gaze the lived experience of a symbolically mediated human relationship as it passes from Real to reality. As the audience, we play the role of Big Other. The commitment of our gaze is what guarantees that these snippets of life, however they're captured, will be granted social meaning, and thus be said to have been worth living in the end.

Chapter 4

The Dialectic of Fiction

In 2014, a *New York Times* piece considered whether prestige television had gotten so good that novels were history.[39] Following the elevation of television to new levels of critical appreciation, it's become common in the contemporary cultural conversation to answer that question in the affirmative. It should come as no surprise that television shows are already widely considered the new novels; after all, people are reading less than ever[40] at the same time that streaming video content has become so inescapably available. While this supposed "golden age of TV" is most heavily associated with fiction shows like *Mad Men, Breaking Bad,* and *Game of Thrones,* it has also occurred within the context of the rising and continued popularity of reality television. As fiction readers leave books for television, television leaves fiction for reality. And meanwhile, prose fiction too has begun its own turn toward the real.

Jonathan Franzen has been one of the most voracious defenders of prose fiction in its classical form and continues to insist on the essential social role it plays. For a writer like Franzen, fiction is important for all of the same reasons that creativity might be important, but he attaches special significance to fiction's fictiveness. It's not just storytelling that is so crucial for writers and critics like Franzen, but specifically those stories that we make up.

In his essay "On Autobiographical Fiction," Franzen reflects on the extent to which real life can inform a worthwhile work of fiction.[41] He noted that in his own work, scenes lifted from real life "rarely seem to work in a novel." They're either too embarrassing, too boring, or more simply, "they don't seem quite relevant to the story I'm trying to tell." From here Franzen offers the rather dialectical remark that the only truly autobiographical novels are those that are the product of intense imagination. Citing Franz Kafka's intimate surrealism, Franzen argues that for a truly engaged writer of literary fiction, focused imagination can be more autobiographical than mere documentation. "What is fiction, after all, if not a kind of purposeful dreaming? The writer works to create a dream that is vivid and has meaning, so that the reader can then vividly dream it and find meaning." For Franzen, this deliberate dreaming is autobiographical in the sense that it is an artistically and philosophically genuine representation of the writer's internal life. Living here is not merely a succession of facts, and its representation cannot be accounted for simply by recordation; rather, to live life is to search for meaning in those facts. Crucially, "the deeper the writer digs for meaning, the more the random particulars of the writer's life become impediments to deliberate dreaming."

But more recently, Franzen himself has observed and admitted to a new weariness with pure imagination in literature. In a more recent essay, Franzen wrote:

Literary fiction itself is looking more and more like essay. Some of the most influential novels of recent years, by Rachel Cusk and Karl Ove Knausgaard, take the form of self-conscious first-person testimony to a new level. Their more extreme admirers will tell you that imagination and invention are outmoded contrivances; that to inhabit the subjectivity of a character unlike the actor is an act of appropriation, even colonialism; that the only authentic and politically defensible mode of narrative is autobiography.[42]

In part, Franzen's concern springs from the manner in which the personal identity, and thus the moral authenticity, of a speaker seems to swallow and animate the speaker's message nowadays. Rather than universal ideas and abstract political thought leading the way, today identity and injury are prime prerequisites to worthwhile speech. This is the criticism often leveled against so-called identity politics, a disappointing but nonetheless inescapable discourse that sets the personal attributes of a speaker above the disembodied substance of their message. Franzen himself has been the target of frequent identitarian blowback—canceled and recanceled over and over again for his passé white-maleness—and in this connection his observations about the declining relevance of pure fiction alongside the rise of identity politics are not only understandable, but all the more poignant.

* * *

Another writer and literary critic, David Shields, has taken Franzen's anxieties and reshaped them into a full-blown ideology. In his 2010 book *Reality Hunger*, Shields assembled a bricolage manifesto on what he calls reality-based art. While Franzen seems destined to lament the demise of pure fiction and tend to its ongoing postmortem, Shields is over it. In particular, Shields takes aim at the novel in its classical, Dickensian, nineteenth-century form: a fully fictional work that nonetheless aspires to encapsulate a broad, shared social experience. For Shields, all of the most interesting expression happening today is taking precisely the opposite track, offering up bits of highly subjective experience in modes that tend to disregard or explode the distinction between fact and fiction.

Shields observes the painful irrelevancy of fiction novels in today's milieu, but goes further in his reality-based fundamentalism. For Shields, reality-based art is human expression par excellence. The story of human expression might have gestated in the imaginary register, but in its mature phase creativity takes up a gradual march toward reality. On the first page he declares grandly, "Every artistic movement from the beginning of time is an attempt to figure out a way to smuggle more of what the artist thinks is reality into the work of art."[43] In a mosaic of aphorisms, riffs, and appropriated quotations, Shields frantically documents this tendency across a broad swath of artistic expression, championing those creators today "who are breaking larger and larger chunks of 'reality' into their work." Among these works he cites creative nonfiction, documentary film, stand-up comedy, hip hop samples, appropriation art, social media, and of course, reality television.

Alongside Shields's patchwork of reality-based art and expression, we might also consider the many other forms of pseudo-reality that occupy us nowadays. Consider the role of streaming docu-series in reshaping and reintegrating into the popular consciousness already-well documented incidents from decades ago, from the Rajneeshees to O.J. Simpson to Lorena Bobbitt. Note the parasocial popularity of discussion-based podcasts and their role in insularizing and fragmenting public perception; this, alongside the widespread political junkyism performed in simulative social media environments, leading to interminable bouts of "extremely online" factionalism and feuding. In the realm of sexuality, already in the early 1990s, Catharine MacKinnon was arguing that "pornography does not simply express or interpret experience; it substitutes for it. Beyond bringing a message from reality, it stands in for reality."[44] Today, streaming porntube sites constitute vast, practically unknowable phantasmic terrains, simulating and in many cases exceeding physical sexual activity in their intimacy with the subject.

Consistent with Shields's argument, all of these formats function to harness and amplify direct experience, trading a highly mediated and curated form of reality for the real thing. Today we increasingly find entertainment, as well as socialization and personal meaning, not through an escape to fantasy so much as by discovering new and dynamic frameworks for structuring, restructuring, and aestheticizing our own reality.

Shields opens his chapter on reality television by noting its linked origins with the novel. CBS's premier of *Survivor* in 2000 is commonly remembered for inaugurating the reality television era. *Survivor* itself was derived from a Swedish show called *Expedition Robinson*. The Swedish show was intended as an explicit homage to Daniel Defoe's eighteenth-century novel *Robinson Crusoe*, widely cited as the first English-language novel and a turning point in the birth of modern literary form. And further still—would you believe it—Defoe's novel itself was based on a true story.

Though Shields only gestures at it in passing, this peculiar synchronicity is of crucial importance to the present work. It opens up a historical dialectic that begins with real life, is met with its fictionalization, and then proceeds to the sublation of the two in reality television. In *Survivor* and the beginnings of reality television as we know it, we see the birth of the novel restaged, its form de-fictionalized and re-sublimated into something entirely new: a higher form of storytelling.

Rather than reducing this creative hunger for reality to an emergent hallmark of the postmodern media landscape, as Baudrillard would, Shields points out that our thirst for reality isn't necessarily a new thing. Rather, he considers it a broad historical tendency, tracing reality-based art at least as far back as the Bible. Shields conceives of storytelling, creativity, and expression as a progressive intermingling of fiction and reality. The historical purpose of art is precisely to disintegrate that barrier.

In place of that hard distinction, Shields proposes a continuum, with high fantasy on one end and the mechanical recordation of physical actions on the other. Daring works of literature, art, and entertainment oscillate in the space between, often staking out one end only to better imitate the other; say, autobiographical fiction by way of creative nonfiction. There's a reason novelists blush when asked about whether there are personal truths hidden in their fiction. It's not because they feel caught or embarrassed; rather, it's because the question so badly misses the point that it can only be met with light, patronizing bullshit.

In a striking example, Shields considers the literary hoaxes of JT Leroy and James Frey, two writers that sold pure fiction as autobiography. These incidents are symptomatic of a culture enamored with creative reality, not only because of the writers' overpowering temptation to pass off their fiction as a document of real life, but also because of the public's extreme sense of betrayal upon learning of the truth. That these were novels of imagination, and not records of real life, they became ugly and reviled in retrospect. Shields remarks that this outrage "has to do with the culture being embarrassed at how much it wants the frame of reality and, within that frame, great drama." The same emotional response can be found in the professional wrestling community and its cherished ethic of "kayfabe." What constitutes professional wrestling as such is the radical embrace of suplexes and power-bombs as unquestionably authentic feats of athletic achievement. To a wrestling fan, calling it fake only means that you were never really watching in the first place.

Shields suggests an inverse relationship between our respective appetites for fiction and reality. In a society characterized by an excessively direct, unmediated relationship to material reality, our thirst for fantasy would be much higher. In a word, we'd be looking for a simple escape. But today, we tend to find ourselves living the opposite extreme, playacting our way through an excessively artificial and phantasmic world. In this Baudrillardian simulation, we're too busy living our lies to stomach any more of them in our art. Structuring creative expression around a hard core of the real helps steel ourselves against the gnawing emptiness of that day-to-day imposterism that three-quarters of us experience. If our own lives are already animated and suffused by living fictions, then a turn toward pure imagination can do little for us. By contrast, Shields elaborates on what reality-based art can do to break that impasse:

> I want the contingency of life, the unpredictability, the unknowability, the mysteriousness, and these are best captured when the work can bend at will to what it needs: fiction, fantasy, memoir, meditation, confession, reportage...I find it nearly impossible to read a contemporary novel that presents itself unself-consciously as a novel, since it's not clear to me how such a book could convey what it feels like to be alive right now.

And that is precisely why reality television has emerged as the great popular art form of our time. Unlike pure fiction vehicles, it's the shade of popular entertainment that best conveys how living life seems to us right now. Reality television feels phenomenologically familiar: strangely intimate and external at the same time—"extimate" is the word. It doesn't hasten to make a positive statement about what it means to be human, but rather stifles that impulse in favor of showing us something we'll already recognize to be unmistakably so.

In a recent essay in the *New Yorker*, Katy Waldman described how literary fiction remains trapped in its own dialectic, caught between its dual loyalties to representational fidelity and authentic creativity.[45] You either write a story with no thread to reality, and thus estrange the work from humanity, or you steal portions of someone's real life—your own, your family's, or something you read in a magazine—and fail to contribute anything new to reality. In trying to sort the two, Waldman encountered stakes that were "less aesthetic or ethical than metaphysical." Ultimately, calibrating the ontological foundations of storytelling remains elusive to us, "like sticking your hands through ghosts."

In its literary dimension, reality television emerges from this dialectic of fiction and its irreducibility to fact or imagination. In this sense, one watches reality television for all the same reasons one might pick up a novel. At its best, reality television is that special kind of reflexive entertainment that succeeds in making us feel recognized and welcome in all our human mania, frailty, and stupidity. Great novels can do that too, as they have done for centuries. But with respect to both Charles Dickens and Jonathan Franzen, it's lived reality that seems to be doing all the best writing lately.

Chapter 5

The Hills Did Not Take Place

Reality television shows are ceaselessly accused of being staged. And many, maybe most, of them are, to varying extents. But on MTV, *The Hills* was the show that pushed the complex artifice of televised life to its limits.

If one didn't know better, *The Hills* was at times indistinguishable from scripted programming. Each episode opened with a narrative voiceover, introducing and contextualizing the episode's forthcoming content. Departing from standard reality television practice, the show dispensed with interstitial confessional segments, instead cultivating a sense of continuous diegetic consistency. Episodes were briskly paced and tightly structured, featuring a chain of clean, to-the-point scenes punctuated by an endlessly recurrent pop-punk soundtrack. Unlike many other mainstream docu-soaps, such as the various *Real Housewives* shows or *Keeping up with the Kardashians*, there was very little downtime. Every scene was focused on hitting story beats, with precious little time spent on quotidian interludes like shopping, goofing off, or dull domesticities. Instead, every episode of *The Hills* was densely arranged, always focused on establishing conflict, characterization, and narrative action. And each episode would conclude with the same wistful music montage and sprawling aerial shots.

All of these considered features came together to make *The Hills* one of the most compelling entries in reality television history. But its seeming artificiality goes well beyond its formal features. *The Hills* is also unique among reality shows in that its core cast has since declared the show to be, in one way or another, fake. Multiple cast members — including Lauren Conrad, Heidi Montag, Spencer Pratt, Kristin Cavallari, and Audrina

Patridge—have all admitted to the show's many shameless contrivances, from faked phone calls to an entirely staged living environment.[46]

A decade after the series wrapped, Spencer Pratt told *Interview* magazine that he and Heidi had shot one of the show's key scenes—in which he berates Heidi for giving him a pregnancy scare—ten times before they got it right. According to Spencer, the cast's compensation was tied to viewership, so they were happy to do whatever producers asked of them to increase ratings.[47]

Audrina Patridge, for her part, reported developing a distrustful relationship with producers early on. After season one had aired, she was shocked to learn how heavily it was implied that she'd had a fling with Spencer.[48] Later, she claimed that producers wouldn't let her go one day until she simulated a fight with Kristin Cavallari. Producers allegedly confiscated Audrina's car keys to prevent her from leaving. After calling her lawyer, she eventually gave in and filmed the scene.[49] Audrina described her overall experience like this:

> In the beginning, a lot of it was real. As it went on, it was very manipulated and guided and you're kinda put in these scenarios where you would show up and you didn't know what you were in for until you were there, and you wanted to run out but they lock the door on you.

Others have reported similarly. Kristin Cavallari and Justin Bobby both said that their onscreen relationship was meaningless, and Brody Jenner said that he never really dated Lauren Conrad. Though it's popular to assume that such statements only confirm what everyone already knows about reality television, in fact this level of disclosure is quite rare for reality television stars.[50] Recently, producers and editors of the show have concurred, somehow vouching for the core authenticity of the show while also admitting to certain dramatic manipulations, reshoots, and dialog-guiding.[51]

As a result, *The Hills* has become a rare entry in the realm of reality television, as perhaps the only show that fully internalized masquerade as part of its fundamental identity and message. The show's sensibility was epitomized by its notorious ending, which begins with a shot of Brody Jenner staring off into the distance. Slowly, an artificial background is wheeled away from behind him; the camera pulls back to reveal a fully fabricated film set. This baffling, exquisite ending is reminiscent of Alejandro Jodorowsky's *The Holy Mountain*, which performs an identical shot and ends with the line, "Zoom back, camera! Real life awaits us." In this gesture, *The Hills* became the first reality television show to hold itself out as openly postmodern.

But because of the show's focus on relationships, the majority of the most glaring deceptions have to do with the authenticity of the desire we see on screen. While some of the show's core romances were either fully disingenuous or heavily distorted, it's less clear what this means on an interpretive level. In problematizing desire in this way, *The Hills* asks us to consider how neatly we can separate the conditions of artifice from those we experience in our real lives, in our own relationships and internal emotional lives. One can tumble down a rabbit hole of contradictory statements by the show's unusually forthcoming alumni, endlessly mining tabloid lore that continues to form a secondary market in gossip and speculation. But rather than parse individual accounts, our concern here is to confront a more radical problem: Where exactly can we locate the reality of desire, and how to measure the actuality of a relationship? What does it mean to say that a relationship did or did not take place?

* * *

To consider the so-called reality of a given relationship first means coming to terms with potential acts of deception. But when it comes to the relationships featured on *The Hills*, we're suddenly faced with lies within lies, the interpersonal truth turned back on itself, thereby precluding any clear account of the emotions or desires at stake.

Consider Justin Bobby's claim, unambiguous on its face, that virtually all of his relationships on the show were fake, and that he was in fact dating offscreen women at the time he appeared on the show. How does that external deception of viewers square with his internal deception of Audrina? The entire drama of their story emerged from his frustrating equivocations and romantic vagaries; Justin Bobby cannot reveal the inauthenticity of his onscreen behavior because he never performed that authenticity in the first place. Similarly, when Brody says that he and Lauren were never really an item, it speaks less to the nonexistence of a concrete relationship and more to the fact that such concreteness is almost always illusory to begin with. The line between simulated romance and real romance can't be drawn so naively.

Consider a more mind-bending example from season four of *The Hills*, involving Stephanie Pratt and a cascading chain of lies that painfully illustrates what Baudrillard called the "vertigo of interpretation" in hyperreal simulations.

In season four, Lauren Conrad briefly dates a guy named Doug, and they break up abruptly. Stephanie then begins seeing Doug behind Lauren's back. This is the first deception: Stephanie and Doug are interested in each other, but can't let their friends know. The deceived parties include Lauren and her frequent confidant, Brody Jenner.

Stephanie and Doug are then caught at dinner together by Brody's mother. Brody finds out and tells Lauren, thus revealing the first deception. When Lauren confronts Stephanie about it, Stephanie claims that Doug boorishly pursued her in order to get back at Lauren. Stephanie says she was taken advantage of by Doug, and that she's since deleted his number from her phone. This is the second layer of deception: Stephanie was never actually interested in Doug, but pretended to be in front of him.

But Stephanie again has dinner with Doug, and the two agree to keep seeing each other. They conspire to conceal their relationship from Lauren and Brody, so that they can maintain their relationship. This creates a third layer of deception: Stephanie and Doug are interested in each other again, but Stephanie has concealed it from Lauren and Doug agrees to conceal it from Brody.

What happens next is where things begin to get confusing. Doug meets with Brody and proceeds to proactively reveal his relationship with Stephanie, rather than concealing it as he'd promised Stephanie. But now Doug downplays it, claiming that he never actually had any romantic interest in Stephanie, and that he has since rejected her. This simultaneously functions as a clever way of preempting suspicion by Brody—consistent with Doug and Stephanie's third-order deception—as well as providing a new statement of his "true" feelings, concealed from Stephanie. This adds a fourth layer of deception, with Stephanie now emerging as a deceived party herself.

When the full group meets up, Stephanie proceeds with her third-order deception of concealing her authentic relationship with Doug from others. Meanwhile, Doug has spiraled off into his fourth-order deception of concealing the inauthenticity of his feelings from Stephanie.

The real interpretative vertigo begins when one overlays the possibility of fictitious intervention by producers at each of the four levels of deception. Each level of deception, if fictitiously orchestrated offscreen, would represent a double negative with respect to another level of deception; a simulated lie produces a truth.

For instance, if Doug were truly interested in Stephanie, then a fictitious intervention on that reality would require a real lie to

Brody and a simulated lie to Stephanie. If the truth was that Doug never had any romantic interest in Stephanie, then fictitious intervention would've required a simulated lie to Brody and a real lie to Stephanie. Likewise, assuming Stephanie's genuine romantic interest in Doug, Stephanie's real lie to Lauren would be consistent with a simulated lie to Doug. On the other hand, if Doug really did take advantage of Stephanie, for producers to instigate an inconsistent fictitious reality, she would've needed to offer a real lie to Doug and a simulated lie to Lauren.

Where, in this dizzying weave of double-negative deceptions, can the concept of emotional truth reside, and where can fiction possibly intervene? As lies contradict and reinforce each other, a dialectic of deception unfolds between the characters, transferring them to higher and higher levels of simulation. Here, the simulative emotional reality of *The Hills* resides not in the possibility of discovering the true, authentic truth of the players' romantic intentions, but rather in the tailspin of meaning that precludes any possibility of romantic authenticity in the first place.

What we have here is similar to Baudrillard's paradox of political terrorism:

> Is a given bombing in Italy the work of leftist extremists, or extreme-right provocation, or a centrist mis-en-scène to discredit all extreme terrorists and to shore up its own failing power, or again, is it a police-inspired scenario and a form of blackmail to public security? All of this is simultaneously true, and the search for proof, indeed the objectivity of the facts does not put an end to this vertigo of interpretation.[52]

The contemporary counterpart to this example is 9/11. Having perpetrated an inside job and an outside job simultaneously, al-Qaeda is figured as both the enemy and ally of American imperial hegemony, its effect and circular cause.

The Baudrillardian answer is this: The reality of *The Hills* isn't constituted by the rote recordation of facts, but rather by the narrative structures that precede those recorded facts and which are retroactively assigned to them. As Baudrillard would've said, "the models come first, [and] their circulation...constitutes the genuine magnetic field of the event." In other words, the drama between Doug and Stephanie happened only insofar as it can be represented and decoded using preexisting models of romantic secrecy, loyalty, duplicity, and heartbreak. But there is no hard kernel to the "event" of their interaction that we can ever firmly grab onto, offscreen or on.

The same can be said of Brody and Lauren, or of Audrina and Justin Bobby. If what we see on screen cannot conform to some recognizable narrative structure—something fictitious in the sense that the model we use to interpret facts precedes those facts—then meaning fades entirely into an abyss. Baudrillard, in puzzling over the way that liberal humanism inadvertently enables the brutalities of fascism, asks: "where is the truth of all that, when such collusions admirably knot themselves together without the knowledge of their authors?"

As the above example makes plain, one can comprehend the aesthetic rendering of social and romantic relationships on *The Hills* only with reference to the hyperreal. The show's internal coherence as a fabricated storytelling vehicle cannot be separated from its role in shaping and contextualizing "real" external reality. Only in this unity can we construe them as events at all, things that did happen, choices that were made, relationships that either survived or fell apart. Try as we may, we can never fully separate the offscreen truth of *The Hills* from the onscreen fabrication of same.

* * *

Did *The Hills* take place?

In the early 1990s, Baudrillard performed maybe his most audacious stunt as a public intellectual, posing this question with respect to the Persian Gulf War. In a cycle of essays now collected as *The Gulf War Did Not Take Place*, Baudrillard considered the ontological status of war in the context of the virtual mass-media event.[53]

In the first essay, "The Gulf War Will Not Take Place," Baudrillard used his ideas of hyperreality and simulation to critique the orgiastic media build-up to the conflict in Kuwait and Iraq. Baudrillard observed that the media reporting on the situation developing in the Persian Gulf was moved to imagine war in a typical sense, as some kind of military engagement among relative equals, and failed to depict it as the obscene fiat accompli that it already was. The language and symbolism of the reporting appealed to notions of classical war—invoking the grand narrative of east versus west; condemning Saddam Hussein as an authoritarian threat to democracy; raising the frightening potentialities of nuclear and biological weaponry—but the vastly superior military might of the United States precluded those themes from ever passing from the abstract into the concrete.

In this sense, the lead up to the Persian Gulf War was already virtual in nature, preparing the public for an event that would never take place in real terms. Tying back to Baudrillard's initial work on simulation from a decade earlier, he argued that the irresistible mass adoption of warlike tropes despite their obvious obsolescence emerged from the postmodern primacy of representation over reality. This was essentially an extension of the same argument he made in *Simulacra and Simulation* about the Cold War, characterizing it as a virtual war constituted by the endless deferral of real war. Crucially, hyperreal simulation is not merely a fake stand-in for reality, but rather a third order of reality that overrules and displaces both reality and its representation. It's within this framework that we now find ourselves socially and politically, reversing the traditional order of things. Baudrillard warns:

> The most widespread belief is in a logical progression from virtual to actual...However, this is an Aristotelian logic which is no longer our own. Our virtual has definitively overtaken the actual and we must be content with this extreme virtuality which, unlike the Aristotelian, deters any passage to action. We are no longer in a logic of the passage from the virtual to the actual but in a hyperrealist logic of the deterrence of the real by the virtual.

In this state of affairs, we no longer carry out war by waging it, but instead by imagining it.

To clarify, the argument here is not that the Gulf War amounted to a hoax; rather, Baudrillard's initial point was simply to remark that postmodern conditions have changed the nature of global conflict itself, and that the media's representation of the conflict failed to symbolize those conditions. In postmodern warfare, it's not force but the immaterial notion of force that is decisive; as was the case throughout the duration of the Cold War, the most unlikely of all scenarios remains the outbreak of traditional warfare. Even as Western militaries continue to toil and die in desert counterinsurgencies, the one thing we won't see is a battle between two evenly matched armies. This is not to say that international conflict is "staged." Conflict is still perfectly actual, as are the stakes involved. But what have changed are the essential properties of conflict and the structural vehicles by which power unfolds.

Of course, contra Baudrillard's insistence on the inevitably of deferral, the Gulf War conflict did come to the use of force. This merely pointed Baudrillard to his next question, in the essay titled "The Gulf War: Is It Really Taking Place?" In this second provocation, faced with the concrete military engagement in

Iraq, Baudrillard didn't retreat but instead doubled down on his mad argument. In considering the ontological status of what was happening, Baudrillard focused on the real-time, round-the-clock reporting of the event to question the experienced global reality of the events themselves. Central to his argument was the antagonistic relationship between social reality and mass communication. For Baudrillard, the mass spectacle creates a situation in which the primary element is not the event itself, but rather its mass representation, and specifically a high-velocity and sensationalized form of representation via instantly disseminated images and improvised media narratives.

The first myth Baudrillard sought to dispel was that modern communications technology enabled us to experience and interpret real events in real time. For Baudrillard, there's a crucial distinction between an event and its mass representation: "What we live in real time is not the event, but rather...the spectacle of the degradation of the event and its spectral evocation." In other words, whatever did occur out there in the Persian Gulf, it was something entirely separate and unintelligible from the perspective of mass media and the public eye, and thus the facts are basically unknowable to us in a traditional sense. This is not to say that the event was unknowable in *any* sense; rather, our knowledge about it should be placed in the neutral context of hyperreal social relations, in which popular symbols generally precede their referent.

The humblest form of this argument can be stated as a simple recognition that the occurrence of an event is radically estranged from the event's representation on television. The latter actually forms its own derivative event, with its own rules, and the original event is left duly distorted.

Another key aspect of Baudrillard's framework is the significance of speculation in grappling with events on a social or global scale. Because the concrete facts are so remote, and while simultaneously the images and narratives supposedly representing those events are so overwhelming and contradictory, our experience of social reality is rendered profoundly indeterminate: "just as everything psychical becomes the object of interminable speculation, so everything which is turned into information becomes the object of endless speculation, the site of total uncertainty."

* * *

Finally, Baudrillard proceeded to his coup de grâce in "The Gulf War Did Not Take Place." His concluding remarks focus on the preprogrammed nature of the whole affair: "Since this war was won in advance, we will never know what it would have been like had it existed." His conceit was to argue that no number of bombs or explosions could produce war as a real event, nor could any volume of media coverage. The best we can hope for today is a simulated war, in which everybody simply pretends that we're back in the trenches. Baudrillard offers the metaphor of disembodied phone sex via hotline or a disappointing striptease; all anonymity and no orgasm. Morosely, he despairs that in hyperreal society, "There is no more room for war than for any form of living impulse."

Though he steps on and off his high horse, Baudrillard ultimately lands in a place of broad indifference. He surrenders moral purchase and absolves himself of any analytic responsibility by concluding that the fakeness of the war was not so significant after all, if only because any possible truth we might've hoped for was fleeting in the first instance. This is how we might say that the Gulf War didn't happen as such, but without alluding to the crude frame of a hoax or scandal: Any ultimate information we might glean about the real event is fated to be just as elusive and phantasmic as any popular lie, so we're left again with a double negative.

"This is not a war, but this is compensated for by the fact that information is not information. Thus everything is in order. If this war had not been a war and the images had been real images, there would have been a problem." But there is no problem because it's "all equally unreal, equally non-existent" and there is "coherence in the irreality" of the entire strange episode. The notion is that, at bottom, we'll find no hidden truths and no revelations, but only a spiraling aporia, the echoes of a narrative feedback loop. Lost in a fog of simulacral meaning, the Gulf War was just one more ship passing in the night.

Is this immature nihilism? To an extent, yes. In retrospect, particularly in light of the ravages of the War on Terror and the bloody geopolitical destabilization that followed, Baudrillard's musings on war haven't aged particularly well. Some consider these essays to be among the worst excesses of postmodern overreaching, and fairly so. But for our purposes, there are more salient readings to mine. The important takeaway isn't his terrible historical account, but rather his warning that the basic rules of the game have changed in the context of mass media, and that many assumptions about epistemic stability and the ascertainability of facts are simply outmoded.

It's easy to misinterpret Baudrillard's work on mass media and popular simulation as moralistic or prescriptive. This is the failure of popular appropriations of his work in vehicles like *The Matrix*, which banally encourage us to "wake up" and see through the simulation. But in fact, Baudrillard's diagnosis is far less helpful. He doesn't ask anyone to disavow simulation. Instead, he recommends we square the terms of simulation with our own subordination to profligate imagery. In a cynical but incisive passage, Baudrillard writes admirably of Saddam Hussein's manipulation of the media, with comments that equally could be applied today to Donald Trump:

> In the West we still have a hypocritical vision of television and information, to the extent that, despite all the evidence,

we hope for their proper use. Saddam, for his part, knows what the media and information are: he makes a radical, unconditional, perfectly cynical and therefore precisely instrumental use of them...We may regret this, but given the principle of simulation which governs all information, even the most pious and objective, and given the structural unreality of images and their profound indifference to the truth, these cynics alone are right about information when they employ it as an unconditional simulacrum. We believe that they immorally pervert images. Not so. They alone are conscious of the profound immorality of images.

In matters of public concern, this could mean an intensified politicization fraught with pitfalls; but in the field of art and entertainment, we need only aim hyperreality toward delight and pleasure. In either case, Baudrillard does leave us with something interesting to say about freedom.

In considering our popular demand for fantasy via mass media, Baudrillard suggests a connection between liberty and delusion:

We have neither need of nor the taste for real drama or real war. What we require is the aphrodisiac spice of the multiplication of fakes and the hallucination of violence, for we have a hallucinogenic pleasure in all things, which, as in the case of drugs, is also the pleasure in our indifference and our irresponsibility and thus in our true liberty. Here is the supreme form of democracy.

What we might excavate from this questionable cycle of writings as it relates to reality television is to consider the uncanny liberty of irreality. Watching cable news or *Keeping up with The Kardashians* might not be so different from dropping acid; but after all, who doesn't like doing drugs? The epiphany doesn't provide for a reassertion of control over material reality, but it does say something about our collective omnipotence with respect to constructing social meaning.

All of which brings us back to *The Hills* and how we might interpret its ontology. Like the Gulf War, enough did really happen on *The Hills* to leave it irreducible to a hoax, and yet its basic artificiality is unmistakable too.

To start, we might content ourselves to say that what began as a half-earnest documentarian project spilled over into an extravagant improv drama recital. At some point, aided by public enthusiasm and the hyperreal stimulant of weekly tabloid coverage, the show's narrative movement became sentient and started performing itself. The turn occurred without the consent or knowledge of its characters and without any particular agenda in mind beyond the aspect of humanity that impels us toward pretense and performativity.

A fair take, but one that does not go far enough toward the investigation of some of our central questions, namely the way in which reality television accurately mimics or emerges from the semiotic construction of social reality and the fantasied charade of personal identity.

The lesson to come out of Baudrillard's mediation on the Gulf War is the same one we seek from our enjoyment of *The Hills*: The proper interpretation is neither to imagine its objective authenticity, nor to place undue emphasis on its fictions. But rather, we can understand *The Hills* to represent something far more contemporary, far more thrilling in its ontological mysteries than any fact or fiction. The interpretive secret of *The Hills* lies in the complementarity of its internal themes to its triumph as successful simulation. Neither fact nor fiction, *The Hills* retains a properly simulative character because its dominant internal dynamics concerning romance are already mired in ambiguity to begin with.

The show's focus is on relationships, both between friends

and between lovers. These relationships are consistently depicted as pending, unresolved, amorphous, deferred, always fundamentally impossible to nail down. And this is congruent with its status as simulation: If we have reason to doubt the authenticity of romance between Lauren and Brody, such doubts only feed into rather than refute the ambiguous arc of their time together. Their ostensible attraction is never quite concretized or consummated, but rather floats ghostlike from episode to episode as a generative potentiality.

This is doubly so for any storyline involving Justin Bobby. His chronic evasiveness folds back in on itself in simulation, and we cannot neatly distinguish between his real deceptions and his simulated lies. In the fifth season, Kristin and Justin Bobby's fully disingenuous courtship extends hyperreal romance to depressing territory. By faking it that badly, their aborted simulation suggests something dark about the vacuity of human emotion itself. It's as if, to exist or matter at all, we must go through the motions of generating love for somebody and performing some level of normative relationality. Those terminally single among us will confirm: To be single is not only to be alone personally, but to matter less on a social level.

If one adds up all of the possible permutations of desire on *The Hills*—that which was instigated versus that which was real, the successful simulations brought to account alongside those that failed—one can only conclude that all of it was "simultaneously true." The possibility of authentic, spontaneous desire is lost, fragmented, and refracted in hyperreality. But to merely blame the show's narrative excesses is to mistakenly assume the clean integrity of desire in the first place. Any such notion of a genuine, uncontaminated, straightforward desire is generally refuted not only by a century of psychoanalytic thought, but by common experience as well. Following Baudrillard's aloof remarks, we might say that there may've been no true romance on *The Hills*, but after all, desire is not desire. Thus everything is in order on *The Hills*, with each feigned flirtation cohering with its counterpart in our own irreal, indeterminate emotional lives. In simulation, romance becomes circular in its ambiguity. Its representation intensifies original uncertainties and generates new ones, and those new uncertainties become further intensified through their own representation. Even where figures like Heidi and Spencer did form a consistent romantic bond, that bond is faithfully depicted as choked by ambivalence and compromise. It is through these simulations that *The Hills* can deliver its most sophisticated affective theme: that love is ontologically unstable. And what could be more realistic?

The Hills told its story in the years leading up to the contemporary digitization and marketization of dating life in the affluent west, via apps like Tinder and its dozen imitative competitors. Today sex is less real and more virtual all the time, as millennials notoriously have less real sex while pornography becomes increasingly available, free, and immersive to our libidinal imaginaries. A quarter-century ago, Baudrillard asked whether war could still take place in postmodern society, and the absorption of war into the hyperreal might be more welcome than ever. But as *The Hills* suggests, this doesn't amount to making love and not war. Whether *The Hills* took place or not, the more unsettling question we should ask is whether romance can take place anymore either.

Chapter 6

Having it Both Ways on *The Bachelor*

Baudrillard's writings on the Gulf War consider whether the concept of conflict can survive the advent of assured victory. If one side has already won, in what sense were the parties ever at war? We encounter a similar paradox of the hyperreal when watching *The Bachelor*. Can love really blossom if the fairy-tale ending is written in advance? Can we simulate romance too? The emotional pull of *The Bachelor* emerges from its excruciating struggle to generate, and thereby rescue, romantic love in the face of its formal erasure. This process replicates the fundamental problematic of romance in capitalism and patriarchy: how to find love within a system that has already rendered it impossible.

On air since 2002, *The Bachelor* remains one of the longest-running reality shows on television. After stagnating for a few years, at some point around 2013 the show experienced an unlikely resurgence in popularity.[54] Since then, its popularity has only grown among the key 18-to-34 demographic.[55] And as a piece in *Vogue* points out, the show is now just as popular among millennial feminists as one would expect it to be among rural Christian housewives.[56]

Viewed in this context, one of the first things one must notice about *The Bachelor* is that it shouldn't be as popular as it is today, when pop culture is more preoccupied than ever with progressive prerogatives. Of the various forms of monoculture, *The Bachelor* is unquestionably one of our most conservative cultural institutions, occupying an awkward "trad" position within a context of mandatory, scalable wokeness. *The Bachelor* can be seen as the leading propaganda apparatus of cultural patriarchy, wherein and whereby family values reign supreme and the mythology of natural monogamy is handed down from season to season. It's a world of matrimonial determinism, heteronormativity, and regressive gender patterns. From episode to episode, a premium is placed on Victorian standards of feminine elegance, and it's perhaps the one place on television that chivalry isn't dead. A private microcosm of virtue, *The Bachelor* is our last simulacrum of courtly love.

The show is organized by a strict moral code. They even have a name for it. In adjudicating authenticity, Bachelor Nation alludes gravely to "the Right Reasons." On *The Bachelor*, the Right Reasons provide a means of moral approval and exclusion, rendering other those not beholden to its strictures. What are these Right Reasons? Mainly, it's of crucial importance that you're on the show for love, true love, and the right kind of love. And as in patriarchy, the only permissible love is the sort of love that results in wedding vows and babies.

If someone isn't there for the Right Reasons, they're cast out like a leper. The show's fan culture rejects any possibility that someone might justifiably be in it for fame, fun, or a fling. *The Bachelor* is a game that's no game at all; it's a performed metaphor for the hallowed process of becoming loved, of fulfilling one's romantic destiny. More concretely, it's a cultural institution meant to honor the nuclear family as an indispensable social institution. As such, a season that ends in anything less than a straightforward marriage proposal is considered a bitter failure.[57]

But at the same time, the show offers viewers a captivating perversity. Its basic contradiction emerges from the real sincerity reflected in its values as they gestate in what amounts to, by all accounts, a decadent pageant of polyamory, deception, and performative melodrama. Here, the traditional ideal of one-man-one-woman marriage is shored up through a surreal, dialectical inversion: In order to find the *one*, you must become romantically entwined with the *many*—at least a dozen potential matches simultaneously. It's in executing upon the clear opposite of traditional romantic fidelity that the possibility of monogamy can be sought after in its contemporary, hyperreal authenticity. Unlike most reality shows, the most important part of *The Bachelor's* rhythm isn't its spontaneity. Rather, *The Bachelor's* drama emerges from its humdrum repetitions. The solo date card, the competitive group date, the rose ceremony; everything repeats from episode to episode, season to season. The process is tied together by recitations of its talismanic vocabulary and bounded by standard-issue smiles. As though engineered by a marriage counselor, *The Bachelor* suggests that finding love is essentially a matter of process. You show up, you follow the rules, and you always lead with your best intentions. Work the program. Suffer its grim protocols. You'll get there.

The Bachelor's understanding of romance as social process dovetails with the continued significance of matrimonial gestures and amulets today. Consider the standard trappings of Western marriage: dramatic public proposals, engagement rings, bridal showers, and all the many rituals that make up the wedding ceremony proper. Intellectually, one can't help but notice the superstition and irrationality of these procedures; but also, we know that without them, love and marriage would lose their transcendent qualities. Similarly, on *The Bachelor* it's through a confabulated formal process and set structural mechanisms that the emotional stakes are formed and then raised. Quaint date setups continually dangle opportunities for preferential treatment and romantic advancement, and then leave everyone else terrorized by the looming threat of rejection. The system is designed so that everyone hopes for a rose but more often ends up in tears.

At first glance, *The Bachelor* seems to be a gross spectacle. Read from a certain perspective, it couldn't have anything to do with real love or marriage at all, since its founding conditions are so antithetical to anything we'd recognize as a "real" relationship. In what sense then is the show so conservative? Isn't this just another postmodern orgy?

The answer resides in the fact that the show doesn't adopt or import any particular real social structure, but rather bows to the primacy of social structure as such. Conservatism on *The Bachelor* isn't achieved by borrowing external values of Western patriarchal traditionalism, but rather by cultivating its own strict *internal* code. The show's internal mores bear only an indirect relationship to our own, representing a certain funhouse-mirror version of what it's like to perform normativity on the outside. *The Bachelor* abides by an exotic set of explicit and tacit guidelines, customs, and taboos, and the lines drawn inside the show are not always, by necessity, the same ones that we draw to constitute sex and gender codes outside the show.

In this sense, the show mirrors, or mocks, the irrational formalism of heteronormativity. Crucial here is the understanding that it's not the content of the rules of gender and sexuality that matter; what's important is that there are rules in the first place. This is the meaning of conservatism in its broadest sense, as a mode of social construction that's less normative and more formal in operation.

For example, consider the odd role that sex plays on the show. In 2015, Kaitlyn Bristowe had sex with Nick Viall on an earlyish episode of *The Bachelorette*. As a result, she was subjected to ruthless "slut shaming" and harassment on the internet.[58] Her decision to sleep with someone she was getting to know romantically became a major plot point of the season, and Bachelor Nation was beside itself with scandal. Producers and editors framed it as a genuine controversy; in the reunion episode, Chris Harrison went so far as to read the mean tweets to her face. Throughout this saga, the show's hardcore fanbase was revealed to be in thrall of a strange, ugly mania. Viewers appeared to be deranged by cognitive dissonance, at a loss to insist upon imposing a code of private sexual propriety on a show defined by its spectacle of public polyamory.

But such derangement simply reveals the power of the show's alien conservatism. Kaitlyn's sin wasn't merely that she'd had premarital sex, as it may have been in the standard traditionalist imaginary. Rather, on *The Bachelorette*, her mistake was that she'd had premarital sex a few episodes too early. According to the show's moral charter—formally unspoken but encoded in each season's structure—the sex act is reserved only for those three suitors that make it to the penultimate episode. Only then are they permitted, literally by formal invitation from host Chris Harrison, to retire to a private quarters cringingly named the "Fantasy Suite." At this point, viewers are left to know but not-know that the Bachelorette will proceed to have sex with three different men in relatively quick succession.

From the perspective of any external traditionalist, the Fantasy Suite ritual would be as degenerate a frolic as any other form of sexual liberalism, condemnable for its indiscriminate dealings in matters of the flesh. But within the show's moral logic, the Fantasy Suite is as sacred a gesture as getting down on one knee.

* * *

Today, our mixed feelings over *The Bachelor* provide an opportunity to consider the status of love and marriage, its future and past, in light of new public assumptions about gender equality and gay rights. When viewed from a critical perspective, marriage and traditional family continue to have a non-obvious place in the Left's account of sexual politics.[59]

But feminist ambivalence over marriage is nothing new. At least since the 1950s, several feminist theorists have understood marriage to be one of patriarchy's key repressive structures. As a result, many feminist writers have exhibited open hostility to marriage, both as institution and ideology. For example, the central plank of Shulamith Firestone's radical feminist utopia was abolishing the nuclear family, and in *Dialectic of Sex* she condemned the culture that revolved around monogamous love. Firestone stated bluntly, "romanticism is a cultural tool of male power to keep women from knowing their conditions."[60] She disputed the very notion of love within patriarchy, arguing that "love, perhaps even more than childbearing, is the pivot of women's oppression today." Firestone insisted that deconstructing monogamy was crucial to revolutionary feminism, as a way of pulling up patriarchy by its roots. "Women and love are underpinnings," she reasoned. "Examine them and you threaten the very structure of culture."

More recently, the concept of marriage has been crucial to the gay rights movement. But totally apart from the homophobia of social conservatives, marriage and family have also been controversial from a specifically LGBT perspective. The fight for gay marriage has been, at times, characterized as retrograde or "assimilationist" by some queer critics. For instance, in 2014 Bruce Benderson published *Against Marriage* and encouraged the gay community to rethink its focus on marriage:

> Instead of opposing that obnoxious institution, marriage, they're fighting to be accepted by it. To me that's the strangest thing in the world. Why focus on a conservative institution connected to nuclear family values that has never respected the separation of church and state, when you can ensure the same rights other ways? Marriage is about family values in the most conservative way.[61]

In other words, Benderson questioned why the gay rights movement was settling for something old and traditionally repressive rather than building something new and liberating.

Indeed, progress and nostalgia make odd bedfellows. In *The Second Sex*, Simone de Beauvoir commented that "modern marriage can be understood only in light of the past it perpetuates."[62] If that's true, the question for progressive straight couples is the same one posed to gay couples by Benderson: Why, even in the face of so much progressive social change, are we still so committed to reforming marriage rather than abolishing it?

From the socialist-feminist perspective, Juliet Mitchell considered marriage's spooky trans-historical staying power in *Woman's Estate*. "For though the family has changed since its first appearance, it has also remained."[63] Mitchell noted that for centuries, marriage has had "a certain rigidity and autonomy despite all its adaptations." The endurance of marriage is particularly glaring from the perspective of historical materialism—peculiarly, marriage has retained its fundamental characteristics even as Western society transitioned from feudalism to capitalism. In *The Origin of the Family, Private Property, and the State*, Friedrich Engels had already provided the standard Marxist reading of family as a power relationship premised on economic relationships. But if property relations changed so much between feudalism and capitalism, why hadn't family?

Mitchell explained that in the shift from feudalism to capitalism, the lower and middle classes lost direct control over private property to the upper class; previously, feudal serfs had been formally tied to the land they worked, whereas the worker in capitalism is fully unmoored and mobile. In exchange, the lower and middle classes were given marriage ideology, which provided "the focal point of the idea of individual private property under a system that banished such an economic form from its central mode of production—capitalism." In other words, under capitalism the nuclear family would function as an ideological stand-in for precisely that which is foreclosed in capitalism: autonomy, individuality, equality, dignity, and happiness. In this sense, family sustains capitalism by simulating feudal values. "This ideology which looks backward for its rationale is, nevertheless, crucial for the present...it rigidifies past ideals and presents them as the present pleasures. By its very nature, [marriage] is there to prevent the future."

Like a good dialectical materialist, Mitchell believed the internal contradictions of the family would serve to hasten its demise. But nearly 50 years after Mitchell made that argument, we can see that's not what happened, neither for capitalism nor for the nuclear family. Instead, we continue to witness the opposite, caught in a web of fascination by cultural entities like *The Bachelor*, never quite sure where to draw the line between guilty pleasures and buried hopes.

So stimulating in the abstract, theory becomes a vexing puzzle when applied to our real lives. In her auto-theory memoir *The Argonauts*, Maggie Nelson explores precisely that tension: the difficulty of understanding tradition as something threatening and regressive, yet feeling moved to participate in it anyway. Nelson tells the story of her own marriage. In 2008, she and her gender-fluid partner learned that Proposition 8 was likely to pass the next day, banning gay marriage in California. The couple hadn't previously planned on marrying, but soon rushed out the door to secure the right they were suddenly in danger of losing. On their way to get a marriage license, they passed anti-gay protestors holding signs claiming that gay people were killing marriage. "Poor marriage!" she thought. "Off we went to kill it (unforgivable). Or reinforce it (unforgivable)."

Which sin was worse? This is the paradox. Nelson was speaking in the context of a personal reading of feminist and queer theory, but the issue is perfectly relevant to cisgender and heterosexual circles as well. When it comes to marriage, do we know for sure whether we want to save it or kill it? Both options feel wrong, and so the best we can do is hope—if not really believe—that a hopeless romantic and a radical feminist can exist in the same body. When it comes to family and feminism, most of us want it both ways, and that's what feels off. But as Nelson counsels, "There is much to be learned from wanting something both ways."

* * *

Sometimes, it seems like everyone I meet anymore watches *The Bachelor*. But no one wants to admit it. Among "educated" or polite company, the first thing that happens when striking up a conversation about *The Bachelor* is that its disclosure as a genuine interest comes with an air of secrecy. Many liberals, professional-managerial feminist women especially, are bashful to discuss their fascination with *The Bachelor* openly, as though it were something to be closeted about.[64] The pronounced guilt associated with the show arises from the fact that its thematic core—an overtly conservative fantasy that posits idealized gender roles as the bridge to matrimonial bliss—is at odds with the official public values of our liberal-professional milieu. Structurally, millennial neoliberalism prefers women to delay familial aspirations and instead focus on career; too much emphasis on matrimonial aspirations might be seen as a professional liability or a sign of unbecoming naiveté.

For liberal-careerist viewers of the show, the question emerges: Why bother? The answer is simple but perhaps uncomfortable to admit. In an age of corporate feminism, gender disorientation, and acrimonious sexual politics, young liberals experience *The Bachelor* as a port in the storm. The fantasy offered up isn't merely the vague notion of love generally. Rather, its perverse appeal lies in the convincing simulation of a particular social ideal, namely one that's more easily conducive to traditional romance than our own, all in spite of the changing times. *The Bachelor*'s unusual popularity suggests that faith in traditional family life has deteriorated so badly that its simulacral nature has become an essential feature of its appeal. Patriarchy itself has taken a hyperreal turn.

We risk falling into reactionary thinking by saying so, but

it's hard to miss the fact that the provocations of #MeToo have occurred alongside a so-called recession in sexual activity.[65] Broadly linked to an overall reduction in relationships and coupledom among millennials, as opposed to a change in attitudes toward casual hook ups, the sex recession has hit the same 18-to-34-year-old demographic that now finds itself addicted to *The Bachelor*.

Meanwhile, dating has suffered a crass neoliberal marketization through a relentless glut of digital dating apps. Urban dating has always been a cruel meat market, but the high-velocity efficiencies involved in swiping left on Tinder have mimicked the effects of other market-liberalization tactics. A dual effect of transactional devaluation and intensified competition renders unbearable everything that was already so frustrating and disappointing about the original transactional form.

Similarly, *n+1* founding editor Mark Greif has written about the ongoing interrelationship between finance capitalism and reproductive decision making.[66] Analyzing the unlikely conceptual relationship between the 2008 financial crisis and reproductive politics, Greif drew a parallel between the monetary black magic of the finance industry and the supernatural reproductive marvel of Nadya Suleman—better known by her tabloid moniker, Octomom. Owing to social trends like sex equality, reproductive technology, and widening disparities in wealth concentration, Greif notes that babies have become luxury commodities for the upper-class and fiscal liabilities for the lower-class. As a result, "Americans have been brought into a system in which they make trade-offs among earning power, individual life chances, present fertility, biomedicine, and cash, in a way that mirrors 'investment' thinking, whether they are rich or poor." In this sense, baby-making in late capitalism, like so much else, has become brutally economized.

In such a context, perhaps one may be forgiven for flirting with the reactionary notion that progress in sexual politics has come at the expense of romantic excitement. But the cultural hegemony—and many would argue, the moral urgency— of contemporary sex activism is so powerful that there aren't many places to give vent to those secret doubts, insecurities, and frustrations about where sex and society are headed. We're not permitted, by social pressure and internal censorship, to admit the full breadth of our ambivalence; to whom but ourselves may we direct the question about whether feminist activism might have unintended consequences for heterosexual romance? Meanwhile, the last thing we really want is a genuine return to traditional gender norms under patriarchy. That, most agree, would be even worse, which is why it'd be a mistake to dismiss this line of critique as merely reactionary. Rather, it can be better understood as part of the price paid to progress.

Engaging with *The Bachelor* means confronting the basic cultural paradox of feminism and sex activism today. While harboring no illusions about the past we despise, we can hardly hide our disappointment with the present. Annulling patriarchy as such risks losing those parts that we're not ready to give up on. The stakes are thus higher than commonly admitted; it's not merely a matter of choosing sexual justice, but trusting it.

* * *

Carol Gilligan and Naomi Snider investigate the question of patriarchy and its strange indefatigability in their recent book, *Why Does Patriarchy Persist?*[67] Gilligan and Snider take as their jumping-off point a more specific form of the same contradiction sketched out above. How is it that Donald Trump could be elected in an era of unprecedentedly progressive gender politics? As Horkheimer and Adorno argued in a different context, sometimes the price of progress is precipitous regress.

Gilligan and Snider answer the question by isolating the psychological function of patriarchy. In short, patriarchy operates as a circular feedback loop: First, patriarchal norms render genuine relationships impossible, and second, those same norms hold themselves out as the only way to rediscover relationality. In short:

> we give up [genuine] relationships in order to have [patriarchal] "relationships," meaning a place within the patriarchal order. In this sense, with its gender codes and scripts dictating what a man or woman should do in order to be safe and protected (as Abraham is by God), patriarchy is at once a source of lost connection and a defense against further loss, a source of trauma and a defense against trauma.

Femininity is based on the formation of a false pseudo-relationship with another person that requires a sacrifice of self. Masculinity, by contrast, is based on a pseudo-independence that disavows any need for human connection. In both these normative gender configurations, the effect is its own cause. Each one maps onto the classic pathological responses to traumatic loss defined by British psychoanalyst John Bowlby: Men embody an avoidant attachment style and engage in compulsive self-reliance, while women adopt a strategy of anxious attachment and compulsive caregiving. Abolishing the mutuality necessary for real intimacy, the complementarity of these positions form heteronormativity, which emerges as the only realistic choice we have to find warmth in the cold terrain of patriarchy.

If this insidious, ingenious mechanism accounts for the persistence of patriarchy, perhaps it offers a similar explanation for the persistence of its pop-culture embodiment on *The Bachelor*. Today, pop culture loudly rejects patriarchy, yet we find its institutional power stronger than ever. Does reality television provide a way out of this deadlock, creating a hyperreal "safe space" to explore our deepest ambivalences about love, gender, marriage, freedom, and connection?

Something is missing from enlightened sexuality today, and for the time being that missing something is made available, in part, through the hyperreal frame of reality television. Our ambivalence when it comes to love runs so deep that we need it to be just the right mix of real and unreal. This form of engagement is not irony so much as a live embodiment of real contradictions. Unlike so much discourse in sexual politics, *The Bachelor* doesn't paper over those contradictions but actively embraces them as a way toward something new. Only this way can we experience a respite from the anxieties of a heteronormative sexuality in crisis.

A show like *The Bachelor* may provide us with the same ideology of romance that Firestone always despised, but the difference is that it allows us to hold that romance at a safe distance. It provides the same psychological function as patriarchy, but rather than having to play it out in our real lives, we can do so using the hyperreal frame of reality television. Acknowledging the contradictions isn't the same as mounting a reactionary critique of contemporary feminist activism; rather, a show like *The Bachelor* is part of what enables the hard work of same, internalizing and aestheticizing its disorientations into a peculiar phantasm of traditional family values.

Perhaps it appears ironic that the contradictions of contemporary feminism would generate enough tension to prop up indefinitely a cultural specter of patriarchy. But to invoke the cliché, *The Bachelor* allows lovesick feminists to have their wedding cake and eat it too. To watch *The Bachelor* is to be many things: a cultural anthropologist, a feminist critic, a cultural satirist, a furious elitist, a hate-watching sadomasochist, or even a fantasy sports gambler. But the main thing you probably are is a good, old-fashioned hopeless romantic. And if you're looking for an excuse to keep watching the show, those are all, simultaneously, the right reasons.

Chapter 7

Who is the Real Housewife?

We can begin to understand her by considering the dual tracks on which the *Real Housewives* shows run. The shows' *domestic track* chronicles the cast members' family life and interpersonal relationships. Here we focus on the travails of childrearing, matrimonial love and dissolution, and other forms of draining emotional labor. By contrast, the show's *entrepreneurial track* follows the same women as they simultaneously form business enterprises and develop personal brands for consumption.

On Bravo, mothers and wives take the lead in their social-reproductive capacity—ruling the roost, as it were—at the very same time they give body to their most businesslike career ambitions. Women on these shows are beset by the demands of the classical double day, but the traditional contradiction plays out in a way that just so happens to work out swimmingly. We see on *Real Housewives* an attractive ideological formation by which family can still be more important than anything, but not so important that it stops you from opening restaurants or founding empires on dietetic liquor.

Within this framework, the Real Housewives form the perfect ideal of contemporary feminism: namely, the possibility and promise of having it all. Occasionally, in figures like Alexis Bellino or Melissa Gorga, the friction between domestic femininity and entrepreneurial femininity becomes the site of gendered conflict and compromise. But far more often, the show tells stories that not only denature the separation between domesticity and careerism, but take their harmony for granted. In this specific sense, these shows have never been about mere housewives, nor can their magic be reduced to a practice in cold business acumen. Rather, the spectacle Bravo invites us to enjoy is a dialectical synthesis of the two: the Real Housewives are the sublated product of the inextricable oppositions of femininity. As ever, the efficacy of this fantasy depends on its complex relation to material reality. To what extent are the Real Housewives real? Do women like this really exist outside of the camera's gaze?

* * *

Outside of reality television proper, the closest we might come turns out to be, of all people, Ivanka Trump. In imagining the quintessential Bravo milieu, we can do no better than the following description of Ivanka's social philosophy, taken from Michael Wolff's *Fire and Fury*:

> The effort among a new generation of wealthy women was to recast life as a socialite, turning a certain model of whimsy and noblesse oblige into a new status as a power woman, a kind of postfeminist socialite. In this, you worked at knowing other rich people, the best rich people, and of being an integral and valuable part of a network of the rich, and of having your name itself evoke, well...riches. You weren't satisfied with what you had, you wanted more. This required quite a level of indefatigability. You were marketing a product—yourself. You were your own start-up.[68]

But the link between this most-contemporary form of feminism and the political Right precedes Ivanka Trump. As Nina Power suggests in *One Dimensional Woman*, the clearest paragon of have-it-all feminism was Sarah Palin.[69]

We might pause to consider that Sarah Palin burst on the scene in the context of the 2008 presidential election, the same year that the Real Housewives became an expanded franchise, with the premier of *Real Housewives of New York City* in March and

Real Housewives of Atlanta in October. Writing right around that same time, Power observed a shift in the relationship between femininity and social authority:

> [Sarah Palin] has managed to avoid many of the old female dichotomies—mother/politician, attractive/successful, passive/go-getting—by embodying both sides of each all at once at the same time. In this sense, she is the fulfillment of the 1980s imperative that women could (and should) "have it all"—the babies, the job, the success, the sex. What can't a gun-toting pro-lifer who beats the men on their own turf do?

Previously, right-wing women like Phyllis Schlafly would only enter public life to say that women really shouldn't do so. Palin, by contrast, was gunning for one of the most powerful positions on the planet; and she did so by playing the hockey mom. In doing so, Palin fused a normatively feminine and maternal image seamlessly with her aspirations to political office. Say what you will about her credentials, experience, and intelligence—all genuine points of criticism—but Palin might have been the first major female political candidate to stake her claim not on being "just as good as a man," but on being something much better.

As Power writes, "Palin is not pretending to be a man— she is pretending to be all women at once, and yet perfectly mundane...She turns maternity into a war-weapon, inexperience into a populist virtue and feminism into something that even the Christian Right could approve of." In this connection, one of the key historical ironies of the Democratic Party is that its own proffered figures of feminist achievement—Hillary Clinton, Kamala Harris, Elizabeth Warren—have all somehow failed to fully live up to the ideal or solve its contradictions, finding themselves caught in the same gender traps and the same patterns of overcompensation and compromise.

Importantly, Power was not so much praising Palin as a vice-presidential candidate as noting the unprecedented nature of her political persona, particularly as it related to the contours of feminism as an intelligible political concept. Specifically, Palin emerged within the context of "a fundamental crisis in the meaning of the word [feminism]." For Power, the Palin phenomenon meant that the term had become so polyvalent that it approached the point of semiotic instability. If everything turned out to be feminist—even abortion restrictions and the Iraq War—then perhaps we'd lost the ability to say anything was.

* * *

Nonetheless, figures like the Real Housewives, Ivanka Trump, Sarah Palin, and Hillary Clinton all convene around a certain form of feminism that is as contemporary as it is controversial. In recent years, it's been commonly referred to as bourgeois, corporate, neoliberal, or simply *power* feminism.

In the first year of the Trump presidency, feminist critic and writer Jessa Crispin published a concise and powerful critique of this strain of feminism.[70] Crispin argued, "To understand how surface-level contemporary feminism is, we need only note that the most common markers of feminism's success are the same markers of success in patriarchal capitalism. Namely, money and power." In the neoliberal era, mainstream feminism underwent a process by which it internalized the very values it had one day fought to dismantle, and as a result lost the ability to imagine and agitate for anything new. Today, the median feminist has become a compromise formation, shedding her radical tendencies and realigning her goals to fit more neatly with those of neoliberal capitalism. It's almost as if patriarchal capitalism itself weren't the problem all along. Instead, feminism just needed a dose of testosterone.

But for Crispin, the problem with this masculinization of feminism was that it failed to provoke a concomitant feminization of masculinity, thus opening a gap in our social and moral fabric. Crispin states the paradox as follows: "In the name of freedom, we broke out of nuclear households to become individuals. And yet at no point along the way did we put serious consideration into creating a social equivalent of the support system those larger groups provided to us." The result is a world utterly dominated by patriarchal values of greed, competition, and individualism. Because these values form a system that is necessarily exclusionary, even among fully liberated and self-actualized women there will be winners and losers; when placed in competition, the latter will far outnumber the former. Here, freedom becomes the freedom to experience loneliness and exploitation, with little by way of care and community to fall back on.

As the German political economist Wolfgang Streeck points out, the mass entry of women into the labor market occurred during a legitimacy crisis of capitalism.[71] The 1970s was a decade in which the relevant question among critical theorists was not whether capitalism was technically feasible, but rather whether it provided its subjects with a worthwhile form of living. Second-wave feminism's "rehabilitation" of the dignity of waged labor thus coincided with the transition to neoliberalism: "Beginning in the 1970s, women throughout the Western world poured into labor markets, and what had been branded shortly before as historically obsolete wage-slavery was now experienced as liberation from unpaid household drudgery." The new influx of "liberating" labor made existing wages easier to squeeze, thus making it more difficult to raise a family under traditional conditions. The contradiction was never addressed by markets, but rather transformed into an impossible standard for women to live up to. As a result, Streeck observes glumly that "women in particular gain social prestige by combining...children and career, even if the 'career' is that of a supermarket cashier."

The critical theorist Nancy Fraser offers a similar analysis of this impasse. Working from a Marxian-feminist structural framework, Fraser's work deconstructs the notion of truly having it all under neoliberal capitalism.[72] Fraser highlights a fundamental conflict between capital and care, identifying it as one of capitalism's key internal contradictions. As Fraser explains, "capitalist societies separate social reproduction from economic production, associating the first with women, and obscuring its importance and value. Paradoxically, however, they make their official economies dependent on the very same processes of social reproduction whose value they disavow." In other words, capitalism rejects or devalues social-reproductive labor and segregates it from the realm of economic production. But at the same time, that realm of economic production relies on it to sustain the economic status quo. Capitalist economic production can't support itself autonomously, but rather survives only by exploiting and appropriating the surplus value generated by social-reproductive labor. Also called care work, even today this labor is most often carried out by women. Sexism enhances the division as a means of reproducing wide-scale economic exploitation, in the form of unwaged domestic and emotional labor.

Fraser argues that this irrational attitude toward social reproduction—by which capitalism structurally devalues the social-reproductive labor it requires to survive—is a contradiction at the heart of the capitalist system. This flaw generates social conflict, the pressure of which builds, and each major phase of capitalism has suppressed the conflict in different ways. In early liberal capitalism of the nineteenth century, the solution was to secure reproductive labor with gender-protective legislation and *housewifization*. In the Keynesian state-managed capitalism of the mid-twentieth century, the welfare state emerged alongside the *family wage*. Now, in the present stage of finance capitalism, a confluence of globalization and neoliberal deregulation has made the *two-wage household* the central condition of domestic viability; a reduction in real wages and disinvestment in social-welfare programs have made anything else impracticable for all but the richest families.

Sure enough, the two-wage household still has a feminist shine to it. At first glance, the critiques offered by Marxists like Streeck and Fraser could be mistaken for reactionary lines of thinking about the necessity of traditional gender roles for social stability.[73] After all, the ability of women to work goes hand-in-hand with financial independence from men, and such independence remains a foundational goal of feminism. But at the same time, the two-wage household has not been immune from the ongoing contradiction of capital and care. Like the social systems before, it has had to find new ways of securing the social-reproductive labor necessary for profitable economic production.

To return to some terminology from the chapter's introduction, the dynamic of neoliberal empowerment-feminism involves a privileging of feminism's *entrepreneurial track* at the expense of its *domestic track*. But that latter half of the feminist ideal never went away. Instead, it merely took a back seat, reduced to skirmishes over access to paid reproductive-planning services like abortion, birth control, and fertility technology. Fraser argues that reproductive technology is designed and promoted precisely to stave off the crisis tendencies inherent in capitalism's dismissive treatment of social reproduction. Fraser cites egg freezing, now a corporate fringe benefit, and high-end mechanical breast-milk pumps as examples of "the fix of choice in a country with a high-rate of female labor-force participation, no mandated paid maternity or paternal leave, and a love-affair with technology." Although these products and services help some women balance family and career in the short term, they're only available to higher-income women and operate ultimately by a logic of profit. High-end commodities cover up flaws in capitalist logic instead of working them out.

As with other bedrock social problems, capitalism responds to this contradiction not by resolving it, but by turning a profit first and letting someone worry about the social externalities later.

That individualistic, privacy-and-autonomy-based solutions were championed at the expense of a true reformation of social-reproductive practices accounts for one of the major historical ironies of intergenerational feminism. Where to go from here? For a start, Crispin prescribes "the act of reclaiming the work and characteristics of femininity that have been dismissed as worthless by the patriarchal system. From the care work of raising children and keeping homes, to the traditional crafts of quilting and kenning, to the stories of fairy tales and folk wisdom." Taking care to parse the feminine from the female, Crispin rightly invites men to take part in these activities.

But more broadly, a transformation of our social-reproductive practices wouldn't be possible if more men took up knitting. What is needed more crucially is broad public support for childrearing in general. This would include free universal childcare, medical care, and other tangible subsidies for young families. It's only through universal public projects and social cooperation that we can move toward an intelligent, socialist natalism.

But in the meantime, *Real Housewives* gives voice to our collective yearning to untangle the contradictions of capital and care. Though many of us know, particularly working-class women, that having it all is as yet impossible, it still persists as the ideal that feminism finds itself striving toward. The Real Housewives, more than any other group of women, are the standard-bearers of that ideal. And like the ideal itself, they're never quite real nor imaginary.

* * *

Is that all we can discover in *Real Housewives* then, culture-industry products of neoliberal ideology? Hardly. While the above analysis hopefully goes some way toward accounting for why these shows are so deeply embedded in our cultural imaginary, it badly misreads the show to conclude that all it offers is an unattainable aspirational fantasy. After all, fantasy is what traditional fiction is for, and we're well beyond that on Bravo. A warmer engagement with the show—unironic, depoliticized, and taking it at face value—reveals a broader complexity running throughout its episodes.

First, the presence of domestic laborers on the shows already reveals that it's not actually possible to have it all—not unless there's somebody else to do the housework for you. Media studies professor Jon Kraszewski has argued that, "Bravo is the only cable station that, on a consistent basis, metaphorically opens its poor doors to televise the lives of servants and servers."[74] A clear example of this is Luann de Lesseps's domestic worker Rosie, who figures prominently on the show for several seasons. As Kraszewski explains, "the Countess needs someone regularly to take care of her children while she attends social functions, dates men after her divorce, and begins her career as a recording artist." But Kraszewski reads the presence of domestic labor on Bravo cynically, arguing that its depiction appears only to otherize the poor and normalize the rich, thereby "win[ning] our consent for the political economy of social expulsions."

One objection to Kraszewski's interpretation is that it attributes far too much agency to producers and editors, requiring us to imagine them opting for a complex sociopolitical undertaking when simply rendering the poor invisible has always been the most efficient strategy for normalizing affluence. In other words, if the goal were to normalize affluence and erase its supports in class subordination, why not just edit out Rosie entirely?

An equally reasonable interpretation would be to consider that domestic laborers appear alongside the Real Housewives simply because they're authentically present in these women's lives, almost ubiquitously. So important are domestic laborers in the Real Housewives' lives, that it'd be logistically difficult to edit them out; rather than erasing Rosie, Bravo chooses the path of least resistance to generate an accurate document of how class really looks and functions for women who "have it all." In other words, Rosie is depicted as playing a crucial role in creating the conditions of possibility for Luann's fabulous life because she really does play that role, as do countless other immigrant women like her.

As Fraser notes, a fixture of the contemporary bourgeoisie is the continuous outsourcing of social-reproductive labor further and further down the ladder of economic class. The capacity of women in each economic class to have it all depends largely on the social-reproductive labor of the economic class below. This happens most directly when upper-class professionals hire migrant nannies and housekeepers in order to pursue careers, forming what Fraser calls "global care chains." Care chains also form indirectly through the availability of low-priced household commodities, which are often produced by the sweatshop labor of women in the global south.[75] In those countries, the intersection of emigrant care work and local sweatshop labor has a detrimental effect on local social-reproductive capacities. The necessary care work is then carried out by poorer and poorer women in those countries, and so on down the line, until there are no more poor women to rely on, so that children and the elderly simply go uncared for. As Crispin suggested, and contrary to some of the more sci-fi expectations of utopian radical feminism, the liberation of American women from household drudgery didn't make that drudgery disappear. It just put the mop in a poorer woman's hands. And as figures like Rosie show, Bravo has few qualms about rendering that reality explicit.

Second, what's important to understand about *Real Housewives* is that as much as it leads with the plenitude of material wealth, what soon follows are its hidden poverties. Many *Real Housewives* arcs follow a familiar pattern. What begins as naiveté, shallow appearances, or an excess of privilege soon gives way, little by little, to hysterical despair and alienation. Read seriously, *Real Housewives* doesn't depict upper-class life as being free of worry or an endless stream of indulgences. True, the typically attractive features of wealth are always present and homed in on by producers. But the show's real narrative energy resides in the violent eruptions that mar and distort those luxuries. The most continuous theme to be found on *Real Housewives* isn't one of harmony or minimization, but rather an orientation toward interpersonal life as a site of live, ongoing, and ultimately irresolvable conflict. To clarify, these conflicts generally aren't those generated by the friction between domesticity and careerism; rather, interpersonal conflict emerges as a much broader condition, native to all human relationships, and most intense among the cast members themselves.

As the intro sequence rolls and the women recite their signature taglines, it's easy to see them as the same invincible, inscrutable feminine power-ideal of, say, Beyoncé or Michelle Obama. Early episodes typically start off with shopping sprees and cocktail parties. The women are shown flaunting their riches from scene to scene, often straight-up bragging about their wealth and frivolity. When they go shopping for the cameras, Bravo sometimes goes so far as to display onscreen the outrageous prices they pay for jewelry and clothing.

But give it a few seasons, and the diamonds turn to tears. As the episodes wear on, those statuesque figures start to wilt and drip, more closely resembling the overexposed neurotic at the center of Woody Allen's *Blue Jasmine* (2013) than the superwoman we imagine Beyoncé to be. Crucially, Bravo's instinct is never to paper over the ugliness lurking beneath the surface of bourgeois life; rather, the show indulges our urge to expose it. The only motivation we need to explain such a preference is that it makes for a more compelling show. As a result, if you actually watch them, reality shows generally don't read very well as functional class propaganda.

The first two seasons of *Real Housewives of Beverly Hills* are the pinnacle of the form in this regard. These 41 episodes are overwhelming for the speed and ferocity with which certain figures fall from grace. Taylor Armstrong's story remains the darkest one told throughout the many franchises. Only a handful of episodes stand between her glitzy life of high-end consumerism and her subsequent tragedies. In one episode, she tries on expensive dresses gleefully in her bedroom, gushing with delight at how wonderful her husband is to buy things for her. A few episodes later, viewers are devastated to learn the real story with her husband: one of severe domestic abuse, madness, and suicide.

Another iconic arc is that of Teresa Giudice, who holds the ignominious title of being the only Real Housewife to land herself in federal prison. But to understand the significance of her story, we must first place *Real Housewives* within recent economic history. A fascinating historical accident of *Real Housewives* is that it was conceived of, in all its bourgeois frivolity, right upon the bubble of the mid-aughts real estate market. Many of the central shows in the franchise were filmed or debuted before, during, and amid the fallout of the 2008 financial crisis, and the default profession of most shows' husbands is real estate. The exuberance and excess of the pre-crisis period fed into the show's foundational sensibility, creating an aesthetic grammar of diamonds and rosè that never went away. But just as the show formed that identity, a global crisis erupted. The financial markets slid into turmoil just as the personal lives of the Real Housewives underwent their own ruptures and breaks. As cracks formed across both levels, a much deeper complexity revealed itself.

The connection between reality television and financialization is apt, as the latter is yet another way our feet have left the ground in recent decades. To make a long story short, financialization has been a process that began in roughly the 1980s, characterized by the growing role of finance in supplementing corporate profits across the economy. As French economist Cedric Durand defines it, financialization is "distinguished by the accumulation of drawing rights over values that are yet to be produced."[76] Finance capital is "fictitious" in the sense that it corresponds to hypothetical value, accounting for productive economic activity that has yet to, and may never, come into existence.

In the 1970s, traditional business capitalists experienced a crisis of profit, by which returns on mere labor exploitation and commodity production fell precipitously. This necessitated a break with the so-called "real economy" and led to a new reliance on financial returns to bolster profits. This new role of finance— what Marx referred to as fetish capital or fictitious capital—has taken root in its own hyperreal register. Durand describes this as a "game of mirrors of financial subjectivities."

In the third volume of *Capital*, Marx said that finance turned everything "into a mere phantom of the mind." As a result, throughout the era of financialization and up until the financial crisis, securities and derivatives seemed to exhibit a magical, otherworldly generative power. On the market, liquid financial assets are neither real nor fake; rather, quite like reality television, financial assets derive their occult power purely by virtue of what we are willing to believe about them.

Real or not, financial products rescued a failing state-managed capitalism from deterioration. But that fantasy crumbled in the fall of 2008, leaving in its wake exacerbated inequality, political unrest, and grave uncertainties about the technical feasibility of the global neoliberal order of porous national borders and securities exchanges. The awaking was traumatic. Former Chair of the Federal Reserve Alan Greenspan confessed himself to be "in a state of shocked disbelief" over just how gravely wrong the assumptions of finance capitalism were in the years leading to the crash.

But here is the irony. Since then, despite the neo-Fordist fantasies espoused by Donald Trump, the economy has not gotten any realer. Instead, we have crawled only further into the otherworld of phantom value, in what is now referred to as cognitive capitalism. This is a concept related to but much broader than finance capitalism. As economist Yann Moulier Boutang explains, cognitive capitalism "is founded on the accumulation of immaterial capital, the dissemination of knowledge, and the driving role of the knowledge economy."[77] Whereas the concrete commodity used to be the constituent feature of capitalist dynamics, replicating itself through the exploitation of material labor, today that basic constituent is dematerialized in knowledge that begets new knowledge. This has occurred through a "virtualisation of the economy," by which the appropriation of the intangible becomes the key lever for producing economic value.

Consumer behavior has also shifted and dematerialized as well. Boutang notes, "consumption is also oriented towards technology, and particularly technologies of the mind—in other words those that set mental faculties into operation through interaction with the new technical objects: audiovisual media, computers, the Internet, game consoles." In other words, it is increasingly our much-disdained screens, not our much-eulogized factories, that form the situs of contemporary value.

To bring things full circle, Italian academic Cristina Morini notes that the feminization of labor alongside the rise of cognitive capitalism denotes not simply an influx of women into the labor force, but additionally a qualitative change in the type of labor performed by all workers.[78] Morini argues that cognitive labor in neoliberal capitalism is paradigmatically female, "both in terms of the administration of labor (precariousness, mobility, fragmentary nature, low salaries) and in terms of the contents... (capacities for relationships, emotional aspects, linguistic aspects, propensity for care)." A cognitive laborer typically exhibits "a female tendency to transfer the modalities of care work...and to make them part of the person's professional work." Whereas traditionally the workplace was figured as a top-down, paternalistic structure, cognitive capitalism demands a relationship to work that is better conceived of as *maternal*: "people bend towards an adaptable/sacrificial/oblative position whole which is a cultural feature in the history of female experience."

Knowing this, one can't help but remark on the emblematic trait of cognitive careerists today: the metaphoric trope by which the worker now refers to her most cherished professional project as her baby.

* * *

In the years since the crisis, 4 decades of financialization and the concomitant emergence of cognitive capitalism can be understood as the subsuming of the real economy by hyperreal or fictional constructs. Few figures embody this revelation as well as Teresa Giudice. The resonances of the Great Recession can be felt throughout the wider *Real Housewives* franchise, but Teresa's fall from grace represents its most poignant expression.

In the first season of *Real Housewives of New Jersey*, Teresa holds herself out as the absolute pinnacle of reckless consumption, channeling the ecstatic financialization of the 1980s and 1990s into her own hyper-materialism and shallow dissipation. Things begin to turn sour for her a few seasons in as she fails to form a manageable relationship with her brother and sister-in-law. But real darkness doesn't fall until her legal troubles emerge. By season six, Teresa and her husband are both headed to jail for precisely the same sort of white-collar wrongdoings that precipitated the financial crisis itself: mortgage fraud, bankruptcy fraud, and tax evasion.

Similar to the way that feminist careerism is supported by

the care work of domestic laborers, the house-of-cards nature of neoliberal financialization is revealed in Teresa's downfall to be a feature, not a bug, of bourgeois life. As the economic historian Adam Tooze remarks in his introduction to *Crashed: How a Decade of Financial Crises Changed the World*, the post-factuality of contemporary political economy can't be blamed on this or that celebrity or politician, whether Teresa Giudice or Donald Trump. Instead, the financial crisis must be understood as a crisis of economic reality itself: "What the history of the crisis demonstrates are truly deep-seated and persistent difficulties in dealing 'factually' with our current situation...A posttruth approach to public discourse is simply what the governance of capitalism currently demands."[79]

The early, now-refuted representation of Teresa's hyper-bourgeois lifestyle—her performance as the tanned, vulgar personification of material excess itself—is rendered all the more realistic for its subsequent fictiveness. The Giudice frauds dovetail with the much bigger frauds of finance capitalism. It's often claimed that nobody went to jail for causing the financial crisis. But Teresa Giudice did, and to see her behind bars in the context of finance capital's emasculation was to see clearly at last that none of it was real in the first place.

Chapter 8

Ruling on *Vanderpump Rules*

A typical criticism of contemporary American cinema argues that movies have descended, unbecomingly, from an artform to a program of bland moral instruction. For years now, figures like Bret Easton Ellis have railed against an apparent tradeoff happening in Hollywood: the perceived antagonism between what he calls, imprecisely, aesthetics and ideology. For Ellis, you can't make worthwhile art without lowering yourself into the dirt a bit. But if you're good, you can make the mud sparkle. From this perspective, a big-budget feature that wears its preapproved moral program on its sleeve is about as impressive as an after-school special.

To an extent, Ellis's critical framework is a classic example of the hidden reactionary tendencies of your typical aesthete. His fear is the same one that haunted Nietzsche, who considered great art the only redeeming aspect of human existence and something that must be screened from interference by the mediocre multitudes. And yet, Ellis's crusade accurately distinguishes between narrative works that, on the one hand, openly commodify a social-justice agenda, and on the other, those that shirk any sense of moral responsibility, instead getting their mileage from shock, hollow ambiguities, or unassuming cinematic spectacle.

Today, the entertainment industry seems largely characterized by a crude bargain, one that balances the interests of those eager to channel the prerogatives of social-justice activism against those focused more plainly on raking in cash. These two motives have traditionally been at odds with each other, but no longer. The most recent example of their coincidence is also the most potent: Disney's *Captain Marvel* successfully characterized its billion-dollar payday as a crucial blow to misogyny[80]; this, as critics bent over backward to say anything of substance about its filmic qualities.

In this sense, Hollywood cinema has become a steward, both materially and ideologically, of progressive neoliberalism. Nancy Fraser explains this ideological formation as:

an alliance of mainstream currents of new social movements (feminism, anti-racism, multiculturalism, and LGBTQ rights), on the one side, and high-end 'symbolic' and service-based business sectors (Wall Street, Silicon Valley, and Hollywood), on the other. In this alliance, progressive forces are effectively joined with the forces of cognitive capitalism, especially financialization. However unwittingly, the former lend their charisma to the latter. Ideals like diversity and empowerment, which could in principle serve different ends, now gloss policies that have devastated manufacturing and what were once middle-class lives.[81]

Taking Fraser's concept and extrapolating, we might note that in the high neoliberal era, the slow fade of worthwhile popular cinema has occurred alongside a materially degraded middle-class lifestyle. The last time mainstream American movies approached the status of art was the 1970s; this was also the decade that closed the Keynesian period and inaugurated neoliberalism with Margaret Thatcher's election in 1979. More than 40 years later, we can't expect much out of big movies anymore; but then again, we can't expect much out of economic life either.

By implication, excessively moralistic popular culture surrenders its regard for the precious inscrutability of human experience, by denying its fundamentally indeterminant nature. Put another way, what we lose to bad popular art is coextensive with what we have lost to economic precarity: a sense of belonging, warts and all, to the club of human experience. The resulting condition is, to take the classic word, alienation, and the effect is a new distrust of moral inclusion as a universal path to dignity. What is the proper response to this impasse? Shock cinema? If we want to watch something empty of moral content, why not just watch pornography? One reason this inversion of pop moralism falls flat is that today, even the barest obscenity is no longer outrageous. In his work on postmodernism, Fredric Jameson remarked:

> [Postmodernism's] own offensive features—from obscurity and sexually explicit material to psychological squalor and over expressions of social and political defiance, which transcend anything that might have been imagined at the most extreme moments of high modernism—no longer scandalize anyone and are not only received with the greatest complacency but have themselves become institutionalized and are at one with the official or public culture of Western society.[82]

More recently, Slavoj Žižek similarly notes the impossibility of stoking artistic outrage within our advanced stage of global capitalism. Boundary-crossing is already so subsumed within capitalism's supremely libertine, hyper-consumerist form, that we're left bored by even the most taboo provocations:

> The nihilist dimension of [global capitalism's] space of freedoms can only function in a permanently accelerated way. Permanent transgression thus becomes the norm— consider the deadlock of sexuality or art today: is there anything more dull, opportunistic or sterile than to succumb to the superego injunction to incessantly invent new artistic transgressions and provocations (the performance artist

masturbating on stage or masochistically cutting himself, the sculptor displaying decaying animal corpses or human excrement), or to the parallel injunction to engage in more and more "daring" forms of sexuality?[83]

If Jameson and Žižek are right, then embracing amorality—a total divorce of our ethical faculties from our ability to appreciate narrative artwork—is not a solution. Ellis, for his part, is best known for his transgressive fiction—the bourgeois serial-killer saga *American Psycho* and the cold Californian nihilism of *Less than Zero*—but those books would likely feel out of place today, perhaps even juvenile. We live in an era not of moral evaporation, but of telescoping moral complexity; under such conditions, a straightforwardly transgressive aesthetic orientation is unlikely to offer much by way of a shared, meaningful artistic experience.

Such is the standoff between ethics and narrative art today: how to hold onto one without losing the other.

* * *

The question of ethics and entertainment leads us back to—why not?—reality television.

Typically, when ethics are discussed alongside reality television, we're challenged to justify its deleterious social effects, dissect the politics of its production, or bear our guilt for enjoying it.[84] But these questions are of little consequence to an analysis of reality television as such, because they recycle the same minor controversies applicable to any other form of popular entertainment.

There is no *a priori* reason for considering reality television any more corrosive or compromised a product than any other fleeting pleasure we might discover in cultural capitalism—professional sports, video games, militaristic spandex extravaganzas, trap music—and yet it is routinely degraded by the critical community and shamefully disavowed in polite conversation. As a result, scrutinizing the moral validity of producing or consuming reality television is almost always done in bad faith. "How can you watch that?" is a line of questioning undertaken by someone who does not understand reality television in the first place. In being called to defend its very existence, we are already assuming the question: *reality television is bad.*

Here, let's assume our own question—that reality television is a valid and worthwhile form of pop entertainment—and cut straight to the wherefores: What makes reality television engaging on an ethical level? Putting aside the commonplace external question of reality television's place in a just society, we can better appraise its internal features. Doing so, we can unpack and delineate the ethical experience on offer with reality television.

In terms of its ethical urgency, three interrelated characteristics distinguish reality television from other forms of art and entertainment.

* * *

First, reality television features real people. One of the base stereotypes of reality television is that it showcases shitty people for us to gawk at. But what could be more banal? Are we to assume that there is anything unreal about being shitty, or that normal, offscreen people are not shitty to begin with? Perhaps the viewer, if he's being honest, is a bit shitty himself?

The real picture is more complicated and humanistic. In general, reality television offers an authentic and engaging moral experience because it's populated by characters plucked from our own fallen world and not by allegorical constructs. In their capacity as real people, cast members are as imperfect and confused about how to be good as we, the viewers, are. Going beyond the "sympathetic villain" or "flawed hero" formulae, cast members already contain within them the multitudes of authentic humanity.

Even in the context of dramatic manipulations exacted by producers, the fact remains that we are still watching real-live personalities undergo those manipulations. Reality television production expert Troy DeVolld describes it like this:

> Even on the most convoluted of series with the most cartoonishly contrived scripts, I can tell [you] with a straight face that, at a bare minimum, the reactions are usually real—something scripted dramas and comedies will never be able to give the viewer. We, the home audience, will forgive the outlandishness of almost any premise in the name of witnessing real emotion on screen.[85]

When watching reality television, we never fully enter a state of pure intra-psychic imagination, like we do when experiencing fiction. As a result, we're forced to consider these people as ascertainable, corporeal presences. In reality television, an underlying bulwark of shared metaphysics unites viewer and cast member, tying them to the same moral universe.

By contrast, scripted entertainment is fictional on a moral level; what is permitted in a Tarantino film is not permitted in our moral community. Likewise, the extravagant moral righteousness of Iron Man is an ideal that none of us actually embrace or expect others to aspire to. Only reality television can claim a plausible correspondence with our own moral lives.

Thus, the salient intersubjective dimension of reality television resides in its ability to form for the viewer stronger identificatory relations with characters than those that are possible in traditional fiction. All entertainment involves incorporating something intriguing from outside, but reality television does so with a cognitive and metaphysical immediacy that traditional fiction lacks. The distance between self and show is shorter than in other forms of entertainment. In this sense, the ineffable draw of reality television operates something like the Turing Test, or Philip K. Dick's Voight-Kampff Test. It activates the uniquely human ability to distinguish an organic consciousness from an artificial one.

Thus, the psychological basis for reality television qua ethical experience is anchored in two psychic phenomena: intuitive recognition of another organic consciousness, and our intersubjective identification with it. To engage with reality television is to explore the way empathy helps structure personality and relationships, which in turn lays the foundation for our sense of right and wrong.

* * *

Second, reality television takes a special approach to narrative. Unlike traditional storytelling, the plot and thematic content of reality television is not, strictly speaking, mapped out beforehand. Rather, reality-television narratives are constructed improvisationally.[86] Only after a certain chain of random events have occurred can they be cobbled together into something coherent. Whatever does emerge as the final narrative product formed originally under conditions of relative spontaneity.

Due to these constraints, a certain neutrality emerges as a basic feature of the concrete production process. A novelist or scriptwriter has the ability to design beforehand the worldview, themes, and moral lessons at stake in her fiction. With those in hand, she can fold any and all moral judgments and messages into the story's plot, dialog, and aesthetics. By contrast, reality television producers have much less to go on. Rather than generating the raw materials of theme and characterization herself, the reality television producer must instead choose from a more helter-skelter toolbox: casting, scenario management, confessional cross-examination, film editing, musical accompaniment, and the internal narrative's symbiotic relationship with the tabloid press. As a result, an irreducible measure of reality is at stake in even the most contrived stories. This is why even the worst offenders—flagrantly fabricated shows like *The Hills*, or its even more cinematic descendant, *Siesta Key*—still manage to insinuate a dose of the uncanny.

No matter how "scripted," story-edited, or smoothly produced a given reality show may be, its mode of storytelling remains distinct from traditional fiction, and this distinction coincides with a lighter touch when it comes to moral sensibility. As Professor June Deery notes, "it is important to recognize the dramaturgical and commercial motives of the broadcaster or producer and not assume too much about moral or ideological impact or intent." In short, reality television storytelling maintains a minimum contingency that thwarts any attempt at straightforward authorial intent. Moralism and didacticism are rarer and more difficult to exploit. As a result, when moral conclusions do sometimes emerge, they come across as far less hackneyed.

* * *

Finally, reality television creates an ethical experience by virtue of its perspective and subject matter. Reality television, in its playfulness and frivolity, first appears as a blasé antidote to the stale virtue-signaling endemic to neoliberal pop entertainment. Its shallowness is also its honesty. But at the same time, the intensity of the shows' internal moral atmosphere can't be missed. Intimate themes of loyalty, betrayal, friendship, justice, forgiveness, reconciliation, amends-making, familial obligation, and the corrosiveness of interpersonal rivalry predominate over all other plot elements.

In fiction, morality is a technical element of plot. For example, the hero must choose justice in spite of adversity or temptation, or the villain is born by resigning to moral compromise in the same context. In reality television, by contrast, we might go so far as to say that social morality *is* the plot. For instance, the members of the *Real Housewives* are often depicted to be launching business ventures or hosting complex social events. But these tasks and errands provide only the frame for the interpersonal picture. What is foregrounded is never the event itself, but rather how the participants relate to each other along the way: the insults they fling, the gossip they spread, the decorum they bestow or withhold, and the loyalties they honor; in short, the moral choices of socialization they make.

In this sense, the dynamics of social ethics go beyond informing the show's narrative movements. Rather, the question of whether someone is right or wrong in a situation tends to form the entire narrative edifice. To state the matter most broadly, we might say the central subject matter of reality television is the rightful handling of human relationships. This constitutive ethic precludes a backslide into childish transgression or consumer nihilism. The lesson to be learned from reality television is none other than the foundational principle of ethics itself: It matters how you treat people, and in fact it may be all that matters.

Andy Cohen has stated as much, with respect to the *Real Housewives* shows. When asked to zero in on what makes his shows so appealing and enduring, Cohen insists that it comes down to giving the viewer an opportunity to exercise moral judgment:

It's about human behavior and we love judging other people's human behavior, I think. And I do think that it sometimes is about good versus evil, and hopefully good wins in the end…You know, you see me with them, at the end of the season, and those reunion shows are meant to be like the final reckoning, and it is meant to be, you know, "Will Kelly Dodd take responsibility — honestly — or ownership? Will she take ownership for any of the things that she's said?"...If it was only [humiliation and putting each other down], and that was the only note, I don't think, 11 years later, we would be talking about this show. I think it would be long gone.[87]

Cohen here conceives of reality television as a peculiar type of spectator sport, where the points scored are moral victories and the audience itself is scorekeeper, referee, and rule-maker.

In the field of metaethics, the relevant approach to morality at stake in reality television viewership is called *ideal observer theory*, proposed by Roderick Firth in 1952.[88] In contrast to normative ethics, metaethical theories don't lay out a set of particular moral rules or values to live by. Rather, a metaethical theory proposes to define the nature of morality itself, by clarifying what it is we mean when we say something is right or wrong. In Firth's account, to say an act is right or wrong is first to posit an outside observer, and then to hypothesize whether this observer would approve or disapprove of the act.

According to Firth, an ideal observer would have the following powers and characteristics: (1) knowledge of all the relevant nonmoral facts; (2) a sufficiently vivid imagination; (3) no material or emotional stake in the matter; and (4) "in other respects he is normal."

By positing an ideal observer and leaving it up to her good judgment, Firth's theory proposes an ethical theory that can be universalist and subjectivist at the same time. There are ascertainable, universally relevant answers to moral questions—in this sense, moral judgments are absolute—but arriving at them requires the dispositional analysis of an individual consciousness. The appeal is not to a theological authority or socially necessary set of laws, but rather to the possibility of perfect conditions for individual decision making.

These conditions are imaginary, but in many ways proximate to real human experience: the opportunity for personalized judgment based on all the nonmoral facts at hand; a capacity to imagine the gamut of varying outcomes and the richness of human experience; the chance to have a cool head and no particular dog in the fight; and, maybe most importantly for present purposes, the faculties of human normalcy.

How well does a typical reality television viewer match up to Firth's ideal observer? Pretty well, at least with respect to the cast members being judged. A viewer is, of course, watching for entertainment. But recall that the entertainment itself consists partially in the exercise of moral judgment. In context, the viewer's moral judgment is carried out from a position of relative omniscience, imaginativeness, impartiality, and normalcy. Thus, while not conforming entirely to Firth's criteria (no one and nothing does), the experience of reality television as a process of spectator judgment approximates microcosmically the conditions of ideal observation.

As a microcosm, the viewer's status as ideal observer is established relative to the capacity of the cast members to make internal moral judgments about their own conduct. Put plainly, nobody onscreen can judge the situation, because they are all caught up in it. As viewers, meanwhile, we've been following along quietly, patiently, and from a distance. The question is not whether we actually have every possible relevant fact at our fingertips (we don't); rather, what's important is that by watching the show, we gain a level of knowledge about the situation that simulates relative omniscience.

Similarly, no reality television viewer is entirely dispassionate or impartial, but as remote observers we are an order of magnitude more dispassionate and impartial than any cast member. This makes us, as far as the cast is concerned, ideal observers of the moral conflicts that propagate the show's narrative.

Firth's final criterion returns us to the underlying humanism at stake in reality television. The fact that you are a human being like any other, and not an exceptional or godlike creature, is a crucial aspect of what qualifies you as an ideal observer. As Firth says:

> For however ideal some of his characteristics may be, an ideal observer is, after all, a *person*...Most of us, indeed, can be said to have a conception of an ideal observer only in the sense that the characteristics of such a person are implicit in the procedures by which we compare and evaluate moral judges, and it seems doubtful that an ideal observer can be said to lack any of the determinable properties of human beings.

What are those essential coordinates of normalcy? Firth wisely declines to hazard a precise definition, and we won't attempt to make the same mistake here. All that needs to be said is that, by definition, any and all of us may stake a plausible claim to normalcy.

Thus, reality television neither instructs us on morality nor dismisses it out of hand. Instead, it generates for the viewer a certain raw ethical experience unmediated by authorial intention, opening a space for ideal observation. The moral landscape of reality television is a place of moral scrutiny, ambiguity, and ongoing reconsideration. Though sides will be taken, more important is our ability to take account, all at once, of the many interests, concerns, possibilities, harms, and joys that arrange themselves within the camera's frame, giving us a vantage point that would be impossible from inside the drama.

The opening up of this space of living, breathing moral consideration constitutes the ethical experience of reality television as such.

* * *

While exploring the way in which reality television creates a raw ethical experience through ideal observation and spectator judgment, the best show to watch is *Vanderpump Rules*. One of the most cruelly fascinating and morally corrupt shows available, it's a painful and ecstatic experience with the power to open numerous avenues of moral reflection.

Vanderpump Rules is about a group of waiters and bartenders that work at a restaurant located in West Hollywood and owned by *Real Housewives of Beverly Hills* star Lisa Vanderpump. True to cliché, the staff is composed of models, actors, and pop stars— each of them variously aspiring or washed-up, depending on which season you're on. The whole cast is consumed with beauty, pleasure, and what often appears to be a state of pure wanton hedonism. The necessary complement to this milieu is a personal life packed with betrayal, duplicity, and manic selfishness.

Particularly in its early seasons, *Vanderpump Rules* cultivates a sophisticated sense of dramatic irony. Its interlocking plot threads are generated and sustained by the cast's reliable talent for lying, with the most successful cast members being those capable of lying to everyone closest to them. One little fib can form the basis for epic drama, but *Vanderpump Rules* boasts what seem like dozens of lies per season.

Witness Stassi's stagnant morbidity, teeming beneath an elegant rich-girl exterior and screaming to get out and obliterate every person, friend or foe, she comes in contact with. Kristen is a bundle of raw nerves, animated by complicated narcissism and self-hatred that slowly degrades into something like borderline personality disorder. Jax, a committed sex addict incapable of adult love, is an energizer bunny of cold hedonism, trapped in a hell of his own enjoyment. James Kennedy is the volatile, sadistic alcoholic, wrecked by self-pity and his talent for emotional cruelty. Tom Sandoval is feminized to the point of diabolical, evoking the queer villains of Alfred Hitchcock. Scheana has made an art out of personal delusion, concocting the most implausible fairy-tale engagement in matrimonial history, a union fated to near-automatic dissolution. Tom Schwartz and Katie are the innocent but all-too-corruptible mediators, overwhelmed but fully complicit, like the viewer, in this tornado of temptation, transgression, and despair.

One storyline in particular stands out for the complexity of its moral turpitude. The show's third season featured a painful battle of the exes, revolving around the post-breakup acrimony between Kristen and Sandoval. Late in season two, it'd been revealed that Kristen, after lying about it egregiously for a long time, had cheated on Sandoval with Jax. At the time, Jax was Sandoval's best friend and also the on-and-off ex-boyfriend of Kristen's best friend, Stassi. Jax, for his part, had spent season two in an ostensibly earnest campaign to win Stassi back—after he, of course, had famously cheated on Stassi in season one.

If these interlocking betrayals weren't enough, Kristen goes on to spend all of season three in a spell of vindictiveness, determined to prove that Sandoval cheated on his new girlfriend, Ariana. Eventually, Jax betrays his best friend a second time and confirms for Kristen that, naturally, Sandoval had cheated on Kristen with Ariana.

In this storm of duplicity, it's difficult to discover even the slightest morsel of redeeming value. That marks the challenge of *Vanderpump Rules* to our metaethics of reality television: considering the level of immorality on display, and knowing the role that intersubjective identification plays in our enjoyment of reality television, can we maintain an ethical perspective at all, or is the envelope simply pushed too far, causing a relapse into empty shock and exploitation?

To return to this chapter's opening remarks, one can't help but notice that the ostensible nihilism of *Vanderpump Rules* seems almost to approach that of an early Bret Easton Ellis novel. We see on *Vanderpump Rules* precisely what Ellis has often depicted: a group of shallow, degenerate elites so infested with privilege and pleasure as to estrange them from human thought and emotion. People like Stassi, Jax, and Kristen would all be well at home in Ellis's moral universe, constituted as it is by the dialectical mirror of beauty and ugliness. In an unlikely balancing act, the cast members remain magnetic and lovable even in spite of the interpersonal atrocities they commit. Or, more darkly, perhaps we are drawn to them precisely because of those misdeeds. Whichever comes first, the show emanates an attraction that is all the more powerful because of our own secret reticence to reject or interrogate its ugly underbelly.

For literary scholar Georgina Colby, Bret Easton Ellis's work embodies a similar complexity.[89] Colby "rejects any kind of branding of Ellis as a moralist, satirist, nihilist, or postmodernist." Rather, Colby argues that Ellis's literary technique performs an interpretive *underwriting* function (*i.e.* a ratification, approval, vouching-for, endorsement, guarantee) for the contemporary. Colby's interpretive underwriting is a radical affirmation of the various unjust social structures, empty values, and coded aesthetics that result in the meaninglessness, alienation, superficiality, and selfishness of late capitalism. Colby writes, "[Ellis's] method is not to allude directly to a subjective political opinion but instead, through a process of exposure, to reveal the underside of contemporary culture."

In other words, Ellis's fiction does its real work not by directly highlighting the all-too-obvious hatefulness of the contemporary, but by exposing it neutrally. The neutrality of this revelation is crucial because it creates the possibility of an authentic moral choice on behalf of the reader. We can't truly reject something until we see what it might feel like to affirm it.

In this way, Ellis's artistic underwriting differs from satire and nihilism; insofar as the former directs the reader to an intended "moral of the story," the latter removes the possibility of any moral conclusion at all. In contrast, Ellis's work leaves the ball firmly in the reader's court, where it belongs, in a place of personal agency, ambiguity, and open-endedness.

These are precisely the moral stakes offered by ideal observation in reality television. Just like Ellis's fiction, *Vanderpump Rules* underwrites the contemporary in its own way, and in so doing reveals a rich moral complexity. The show's relational hijinks confront the viewer with an ostensible evaporation of morality, but the daring humanity of it all compels us to look closer. Once the full range of nonmoral facts are taken into account— for instance, the toxicity of Sandoval and Kristen's original relationship, the obstinate refusal of Stassi to grant Jax any opportunity to redeem himself, the self-loathing and confusion that Kristen experienced through all of it—then the moral drama of *Vanderpump Rules* becomes far deeper and more difficult to unpack. The show twists itself into an unsolvable ethical riddle, eschewing nihilism and creating the conditions for committed, continuous moral reappraisal.

In its later seasons, *Vanderpump Rules* has become less about the commission of fresh sins, and more about the question of forgiveness. According to the apparent adjudications of Lisa Vanderpump, certain current and former employees of hers—Jax, Stassi, Lala—appear to be granted forgiveness, and set on a path to redemption. Meanwhile, for others—Kristen, James—access to salvation is, as yet, foreclosed. The seeming capriciousness of Lisa's adjudications give way to the show's crucial ambiguity. The question is ultimately not whether Lisa can forgive Jax, but whether the viewer can. And if, after so many episodes of moral turpitude and performative repentance, the viewer still can't make up her mind about the color of Jax's soul? All that means is that the show is working.

Chapter 9

How to Survive Social Psychosis

In the current political environment, it's tempting to disavow anything that doesn't offer an instrumental political function. The era of nonstop resistance leaves us beset by such guilt and social pressure that even our pleasures must resist, as though joys weren't precisely what we'd been fighting for all along. Cutting against that tendency, the purpose of the foregoing has been an attempt to offer an account of reality television that is mainly divorced from instrumental political concerns, and instead based on a more primary experience of critical contemplation, celebration, and enjoyment.

Nonetheless, it has also been my obligation to frame this account within a particular historical moment, if only because the characteristics of this moment are what lay the foundations for a credible theory in the first place. More than ever, we live and relate to each other in a simulative social environment, one characterized by pervasive doubt, overstimulation, and hyper-signification. Whereas once grand narratives fed us our lines, today we relate to each other only by interfacing with our own fragmented, interlocking personal narratives. The promise and possibility of our political future will depend on how we manage these elements of contemporary simulation. Our principal difficulty resides in coming to terms with the necessarily aporic nature of today's social reality without embracing its most degenerate excesses.

In the interest of moving us toward such a conclusion, a review of Jodi Dean's early work will be crucial to understanding how to navigate such strange waters.[90] Like Baudrillard, Dean's work seeks to understand the dynamics of mass-media spectacle and the impact of instantaneous communications technology on traditional assumptions of shared political reality. But unlike the irresolute provocations of Baudrillard, Dean's work is more coherently politicized and grounded in political economy, psychoanalysis, and media theory.

One of Dean's key concepts is communicative capitalism, which she defines as "the materialization of ideals of inclusion and participation in information, entertainment, and communications technologies in ways that capture resistance and intensify global capitalism." Dean traces our entanglement with "this democracy that talks without responding" to two sets of historical conditions, both involving the role of the Left. Communicative capitalism is founded on a failure and a victory.

First, Dean emphasizes the Left's unacknowledged victory in cultural politics. Waged through the 1980s and 1990s, the culture wars ended decisively in the Left's favor. But insidiously, this didn't lead to the demise of the Right as a species, but rather stimulated its mutation into something fitter. The Left was so effective in shaking the foundations of conservative social values, in trading sclerotic public morals and trust in objective truth for progressive social liberalism and postmodern relativism, that the entire landscape shifted. Dean writes:

> [T]he prominence of politically active Christian fundamentalists, Fox News, and the orchestrations of Bush advisor Karl Rove all demonstrate the triumph of postmodernism. These guys take social construction— packaging, marketing, and representation—absolutely seriously. They put it to work. The right's will to construct (and deconstruct) reality to fit their interests reached new extremes during the Bush administration.

Since then, the postmodern Right has continued apace. The Trump administration is only the latest and most extreme version of a political Right enlivened by fluid social reality. Likewise, the fact that neoliberal economic policies have thrived in the postmodern era is no accident and no contradiction: "Corporate capitalism similarly embodies the triumph of postmodernism. Wink and guerrilla marketing...apply to consumers insights into the generation of affect and desire celebrated by scholars in critical theory, philosophy, and cultural studies."

In its overzealous litigation of the culture wars, the cultural Left found its victory over cultural reality too intense to bear, and thus failed to appreciate the way in which its political rivals were already busy repurposing and weaponizing postmodernism to better entrench their material interests. Meanwhile, progressive forces retreated into a fantasy of their own defeat, rather than rising to the occasion and accepting the responsibility of political power.

This led to Dean's second condition for communicative capitalism, which was the Left's utter defeat in the realm of political economy. Preoccupied by culture wars and scared of its own shadow, the Left found itself asleep at the wheel as Reagan and Thatcher dismantled regulations, cut taxes, broke unions, and sentenced the whole of human experience to the cold machinery of the market. This failure, beginning in the late 1970s and culminating with the perfidies of Tony Blair and Bill Clinton in the 1990s, ushered in postmodernism's complementary tide of neoliberalism. The trauma of this failure, and more specifically the Left's participation in its own defeat, led it to embrace the fantasies of popular discourse rather than to take up concrete political struggle. To this day, the Left remains confined to communicative capitalism and subject to a democracy of cheap talk.

Under such a system, content circulates endlessly and never quite lands: "Instead of leading to more equitable distributions of wealth and influence, instead of enabling the emergence of a richer variety in modes of living and practices of freedom, the deluge of screens and spectacles coincides with extreme corporatization, financialization, and privatization across the globe." And further, the "intense circulation of content in communicative capitalism occludes the antagonism necessary for politics, multiplying antagonism into myriad minor issues and events." Communicative exchanges on Twitter replace struggles for power in institutional and state settings, creating the conditions for a Left that paradoxically gets louder as its political efficacy wanes.

Dean joins these two strands of Left victory and Left defeat— of the coincidence of cultural postmodernism and economic neoliberalism—together in the psychological effects of our shift away from Keynesian state-managed capitalism. Drawing on the work of Jacques Lacan and Slavoj Žižek, Dean explains how the shift away from Keynesian economics entailed what she and Žižek refer to as a decline of symbolic efficiency. This meant that formerly stable identities and social structures were abandoned in favor of "fluid, hybrid, and mobile imaginary identities." In key ways, the subject produced by this decline in symbolic efficiency resembles Fredric Jameson's postmodern subject, which is fragmented by hyper-consumerism and afloat on the dizzying accelerants of late capitalism.

The symbolic order, as we'll recall from an earlier chapter, refers to the outside structure that we enter into when we constitute our subjectivity. As Dean puts it, "the symbolic is what counts as our everyday experience, our understanding of the role of names and offices, our expectations regarding references. We might say that the symbolic refers to what everybody knows." One can analogize a highly efficient symbolic order to an ideal of social conservatism: There are unspoken rules that bind and constitute society, whether or not you happen to like them. And if you're wise, you'll not only accept and obey those rules, but you'll also internalize and identify with them, taking solace in the comforting stability they offer.

As Dean observes, there was a certain harmony between

strong symbolic identities and the Keynesian state. In the most basic sense, Keynesianism offered greater stability to people insofar as it was premised on the reproduction of the family unit via the household wage, and it also emphasized the maintenance of a healthy consumer demand, supported by stable employment. To the extent that neoliberalism dismantled those basic economic structures in favor of competitive marketization, super profits, the financialization of consumer demand, and imperial globalism, the integrity or usefulness of the symbolic order declined. Subjects in neoliberal capitalism were thus left with "no ultimate guarantor of meaning" and the feeling that "we cannot count on something like reality" anymore.

* * *

Dean's account of communicative capitalism and the decline in symbolic efficiency offers some useful insights into the special status and appeal of reality television. Dean identifies the material bases for our destabilized social reality and takes seriously the political consequences of such a shift. But most importantly, Dean's work cautions us strongly against the misguided assumption that the fascinating liberties offered by reality television are automatically consonant with anything resembling a strong leftist politics.

Alongside reality television, conspiracy theory is the other form of reality-replacing narrative now encroaching upon traditional politics. In the Trump era, both sides of the political spectrum indulge in their own form of conspiracy-mindedness. Liberals, humiliated and in denial over their 2016 defeat, conjure coordinated spy games and Slavic boogeymen. Meanwhile, the Right busies itself with twisted hallucinations like Pizzagate, QAnon, and the coordinated string-pulling of a globalist elite known as The Cathedral. By the time the Jeffrey Epstein scandal captured the imaginations of large portions of the socialist

Left, the hyperreal turn was complete. No longer was there any outside to the conspiratorial landscape, but only its interlocking, politicized zones.

In her analysis of the 9/11 "truth" movement, Jodi Dean suggests that communicative capitalism has fostered a public discursive environment that is psychotic in its formal structure. Dean notes that the severity of the "gap between official and alternative accounts [of 9/11] raises the question of the possibility of facts credible to both," suggesting that the polis is losing its capacity for basic epistemic consensus. It's not merely that the facts aren't out there, or that some key piece of information is still missing; rather, there seems to be no set of facts that could definitively prove or disprove any particular account of 9/11, official or conspiratorial. The event is undecidable. Nothing ever quite adds up, and even if it did, that'd be further evidence of a coordinated ruse. The widespread insistence by so many that there is, to varying degrees, probably more to the story of 9/11 than the government is letting on is indicative of a broader phenomenon, namely "the absence of conditions of possibility for something like belief or credibility."

In this, Dean anticipated the post-truth politics of the Trump administration's fake news and alternative facts by nearly a decade. But at the same time, Dean's analysis is careful to take a step back and resist dismissing conspiracy-minded social movements as a passing irrelevancy. Instead, Dean takes seriously the conditions necessary for this "pluralizing of facts and values," as such thinking and communication "has been a key tactic in the culture wars." The mainstream liberal view of democracy assumes the easy availability of truth, and our agreement on the conditions for its recognition. But under communicative capitalism, we can't even rely anymore on the assurances of shared reality. Thus, attempts to place the 9/11 truth movement outside the ambit of actually existing politics, "is premised on the fantasy that there is no fundamental disagreement over the basic character of the world (or that such disagreement has no bearing on politics)." Dean's work urges us to consider that such a presumption is misplaced.

In coming to terms with what she understands to be our new condition of social psychosis, Dean nonetheless dares to ask the dangerous question:

> The proliferation of contents and voices, sources and alternatives, links and possibilities so vital a counter to corporate media's investments in and support of global capitalism—particularly in its neoliberal form—creates conditions amenable to the flourishing of psychotic discourse. Does it make sense to try to learn from them?

As we near the end of the present book, dare we answer in the affirmative?

Dean plays with the idea that after the Clinton years—an era of pragmatic compromises, betrayals, and ideological surrender— what the Left actually needed was a break from reality. The trauma of 9/11 led to conspiracy theories and wars based upon lies, but it also led to one of the most activated and organized left movements in decades, as the antiwar movement took root, and led finally into Occupy Wallstreet. Policy-wise, the Obama years weren't progress, but rather a failed return to the unacceptable doldrums of neoliberalism's epistemic consensus, a centrist daydream that liberal democracy was safely back on the track of communicative reason. This, even as grave reactionary elements bubbled beneath the surface and the climate of post-crisis capitalism grew colder and colder.

In much the same vein, there can be little doubt that our most recent break from reality, the election of America's first reality television president, has been coincident with a resurgent and invigorated Left. Not since the Great Depression has socialism been so widely discussed and its goals so close to being seized upon. If, as Dean argues, the post-Clinton Left "desired shock, horror, rupture, some kind of break with the neoliberal confidence, dot-com euphoria, and consumer-oriented cultivation of unique identities characteristic of the Clinton years," we found ourselves in the same exact position as Obama left office, unconsciously hoping for something that would subvert the stability of a shared neoliberal reality, shaking us loose from the capitalist realism that center-liberalism has continued to chain itself to.

* * *

In much the same way that Jodi Dean conceived of conspiracy theory as symptomatic of a breakdown in shared social reality, Fredric Jameson saw conspiracy theory as a way of grappling with what he called the postmodern sublime, namely the unrepresentable nature of multinational finance capitalism and its telescoping technological supplements. For Jameson, conspiracy theory was merely a sad way of conceiving of the inconceivable, "a degraded attempt...to think the impossible totality of the contemporary world system." Of course, we're all consciously aware of that system: the unseen network of high-velocity digital transactions; financial relationships structured by fractal derivative products; the omniscience of data-mined algorithmic advertising; and the worldwide availability of weapons of extinction. But in fact, this awareness is always impotently provisional and piecemeal, and the totality of today's world far exceeds our traditional faculties of imagination and representation. In many ways, we're adrift in a world we can no longer see.

Jameson thought that the political role of postmodern art and culture—if we can speak of it having any role at all—would thus have to consist in a "cognitive mapping" of late capitalism's hidden landscape. This mapping would serve a disalienating function as it attempted to locate and orient human experience against the backdrop of late capitalism's own absurdity and incoherence. Dismissing the idea that one can ever think or act from a position fully outside of postmodernism—arguing, to the contrary, that postmodernism consists in the very impossibility of such critical distance—Jameson was moved to speculate that the cultural products of postmodernism, bizarre and crass though they seem, might actually be "peculiar new forms of realism."[91] These strange new realisms might serve as perhaps the only chance we have to represent actually existing human experience, locked as we are in a reality that continues to defy representation.

In this humble sense, we can at least provisionally avoid the conclusion that reality television and its attendant deformations of social truth are constitutively irreconcilable with progressive politics. Moreover, there remain ambiguities inherent in our attraction to reality television that allow us to stop well short of condemning it as an irredeemable enabler of neoliberalism. For one thing, we might consider that the decline in symbolic efficiency that has enabled reality-based art and entertainment to flourish also functions simultaneously as a refuge of the symbolic. Witness, for instance, the way that simulated gender roles and romance draw us time and again to *The Bachelor*, as if seeking shelter from a cold, disappointing environment of marketized romance and dating apps, not to mention the many forms of economic precarity that create obstacles to establishing a gratifying and stable family life. Why does *Real Housewives* reproduce so brazenly in its title the contradiction between ruthless careerism and feminine domesticity, if not to underscore the obvious impossibility of "having it all" under present neoliberal conditions? And from where does the warmth we feel while watching house-of-strangers shows like *Real World* and *Jersey Shore* come, but from the alienation we feel under globalized capitalism and its attendant destruction of local community?

Again, the point is not to identify reality television as a site of legitimate political struggle or a font of otherwise inscrutable truths; rather, the foregoing seeks only to establish that our enjoyment and fascination with reality television emerges from all our most human impulses, which haven't gone anywhere but have been put to the test under the historically specific conditions of our time. To engage with reality television in all its foolishness and mania—to affirm its thinly masked pathos and its ambivalent relationship to truth—is to experience just how it feels to be alive today. Reality television is our way of making real a life that is only getting more fictional, and it's a fine way to spend evenings if we're to say yes to the future at all.

Endnotes

Chapter 1

1. Jarett Kobek, *Only Americans Burn in Hell*, (We Heard You Like Books, 2019), pp. 6-7.
2. Julie Miller, "Is Reality TV Really to Blame for President Donald Trump?" *Vanity Fair* (June 7, 2018).
3. Nick Rogers, "How Wrestling Explains Alex Jones and Donald Trump," *New York Times* (April 25, 2017). ("for at least 50 years 'kayfabe' has referred to the unspoken contract between wrestlers and spectators: We'll present you something clearly fake under the insistence that it's real, and you will experience genuine emotion. Neither party acknowledges the bargain, or else the magic is ruined. To a wrestling audience, the fake and the real coexist peacefully... The artifice is not only understood but appreciated: The performer cares enough about the viewer's emotions to want to influence them. Kayfabe isn't about factual verifiability; it's about emotional fidelity.")
4. Jeff Nesbit, "Donald Trump Is the First True Reality TV President," *Time* (December 9, 2016).
5. "Greg Price, "Trump All But Admits His Presidency Is a Reality TV Show as He Welcomes Media 'Back to the Studio,'" *Newsweek* (January 10, 2018).
6. Kara Fox, "'Post-truth' named word of the year by Oxford Dictionaries," *CNN* (November 16, 2016).
7. Angela Nagle, *Kill All Normies* (Zer0 Books, 2017), p. 57.
8. Fredric Jameson notes a similar connection between postmodernism and reactionary cultural politics, explaining how the former can arise from a more specific hostility to modernism; from the cultural right, in the conservative art criticism and New Journalism of Tom Wolfe, and from the Left, as a cancer to progressive Enlightenment liberalism, as

in the political theory of Jürgen Habermas.

9. Jeet Heer, "America's First Postmodern President," *The New Republic* (July 8, 2017).

10. Fredric Jameson offers valuable advice on the futility of bringing stable meaning to bear on "postmodernism" as a term: "for the concept is not merely contested, it is also internally conflicted and contradictory...every time [the word] is used, we are under the obligation to rehearse those inner contradictions and to stage those representational inconsistencies and dilemmas." The present work does not seek to improve upon traditional academic understandings of postmodernism, other than to identify it as broadly descriptive of today's cultural experience and social epistemology.

11. The work of Matthew McManus provides some of the best investigations of this unlikely relationship between postmodernism and conservatism. For a fantastic primer, see his article "The Emergence and Rise of Postmodern Conservatism," *Quillette* (May 17, 2018). For a fuller and richer account, see his *The Rise of Post-Modern Conservatism: Neoliberalism, Post-Modern Culture, and Reactionary Politics*, (Vancouver: Palgrave Macmillan, 2019).

12. Harrison Fluss and Landon Frim, "Aliens, Antisemitism, and Academia," *Jacobin* (March 11, 2017).

13. Aaron Colton, "Why Are We Blaming Postmodernism for Trump?" *The Outline* (August 29, 2017).

14. David Harvey, "Neoliberalism As Creative Destruction," *The Annals of the American Academy of Political and Social Science* (Vol. 610, March 2007), pp. 29-30.

15. Corey Robin, "Nietzsche's Marginal Children: On Friedrich Hayek," *The Nation* (May 7, 2013).

16. According to one study, 70 percent of reality TV viewers say they don't care whether a show is "staged" or not. See Troy DeVolld, *Reality TV*, (Michael Weise Productions, 2016), p. 7.

17. Fredric Jameson, *Postmodernism, Or the Cultural Logic of Late Capitalism* (Durham & London: Duke University Press, 1991), p. 21.
18. Media studies professor June Deery observes that reality television "has put so much stress on the notion of reality that we may not be at the point of referring to real reality... there is a growing recognition of the extent to which we all perform in real-life social interactions—a tendency that is only exacerbated by social media." June Deery, *Reality TV*, (New York: Polity Press, 2015) pp. 26, 43.
19. Fredric Jameson, *Marxism and Form* (Princeton University Press, 1971), p. 45.
20. Alongside my definition, consider also June Deery's "staged actuality" and the following formal characteristics: "a non-fictional presentation of actual events occurring in the empirical world as experienced by amateur participants who have not been hired to act as someone other than themselves or to recite a program-length script."

Chapter 2

21. Jean Baudrillard, *Simulacra and Simulation* (Ann Arbor: University of Michigan Press, 1994).
22. Joe Langford and Pauline Rose Clance, "The Imposter Phenomenon," *Psychotherapy* 30 (Fall 1993).
23. Abigail Abrams, "Yes, Imposter Syndrome is Real. Here's How to Deal with It," *Time* (June 20, 2018).
24. Jameson, *Postmodernism*, pp. 14-15.
25. Jameson, *Marxism and Form*, p. 28.
26. Quoted in DeVolld, *Reality TV*, p. 13.
27. Baudrillard, *Simulacra*, p. 28.

Chapter 3

28. Lili Anolik, "How O.J. Simpson Killed Popular Culture." *Vanity Fair* (May 7, 2014).

29. Robin Young, "Andy Cohen on 'Housewives,' Late-Night Talks and His Disagreement with Gloria Steinem," WBUR (January 4, 2017).
30. Matthew Gertz, "I've Studied the Trump-Fox Feedback Loop for Months. It's Crazier than You Think," *Politico* (January 5, 2018).
31. Slavoj Žižek, *How to Read Lacan* (W. W. Norton & Company, 2007).
32. Slavoj Žižek, "The Big Other Doesn't Exist," *Journal of European Psychoanalysis* (Spring-Fall 1997).
33. Slavoj Žižek, "God as the Big Other," *Lacanian Ink* 40 (2012).
34. See DeVolld, *Reality TV*, pp. 69-97.
35. Slavoj Žižek, *Looking Awry*, 74.
36. Mark Fisher, "Gothic Oedipus: Subjectivity and Capitalism in Christopher Nolan's *Batman Begins*," *K-Punk* (ed. Darren Ambrose) (Repeater Books, 2018).
37. Slavoj Žižek, *The Plague of Fantasies* (New York: Verso, 1997), pp. 36-40.
38. Troy DeVolld, *Reality TV*, pp. 7-8.

Chapter 4

39. Adam Kirsch and Mohsin Hamid, "Are the New 'Golden Age' TV Shows the New Novels?" *New York Times* (February 25, 2014).
40. Christopher Ingraham, "Leisure reading in the US is at an all-time low," *The Washington Post* (June 29, 2018).
41. Jonathan Franzen, "On Autobiographical Fiction," *Farther Away: Essays* (New York: Farrar, Straus & Giroux, 2012), p. 119.
42. Jonathan Franzen, "The Essay in Dark Times," *The End of the End of the Earth: Essays* (New York: Farrar, Straus & Giroux, 2018), p. 3.
43. David Shields, *Reality Hunger* (New York: Vintage Books, 2010), p. 1.

44. Catharine MacKinnon, *Only Words* (1993), p. 25.

45. Katy Waldman, "Who Owns a Story?" *New Yorker* (April 17, 2019).

Chapter 5

46. Notoriously, Lauren Conrad was not on the other end of the phone when Spencer called to apologize. Additionally, the home that Heidi and Spencer are depicted as living in during season five was not, in fact, their home at all. It belonged to somebody else entirely, and served them only as a set.

47. Elliott David, "Nearly a Decade Later, The Hills Comes Back to Reality," *Interview* (February 21, 2019).

48. Lauren Brown, "7 Story Lines on The Hills That Were Actually Totally Fake," *Glamour* (May 24, 2016).

49. Desiree Murphy, "'The Hills' Cast Celebrates 10 Year Anniversary by Revealing the Reality Show's 7 Fakest Storylines," *ET* (May 23, 2016).

50. See DeVolld, *Reality TV*, pp. 20-21 (noting *The Hills* as an exceptional example of staginess).

51. For a contradictory collection of perspectives from the erstwhile production crew, see Joe-Marie McKenzie, "'The Hills': Was It Real or Fake? Creators Take Sides 10 Years Later," *ABC News* (May 31, 2016).

52. Baudrillard, *Simulacra and Simulation*, 16.

53. Jean Baudrillard, *The Gulf War Did Not Take Place* (Sydney: Power Publications, 1995), p. 27.

Chapter 6

54. Amy Chozick and Bill Carter, "After a Rough Patch, 'The Bachelor' Wins Back Viewers," *New York Times* (March 10, 2013).

55. See Sandra Gonzalez, "For 'Bachelor' Viewers, the 'Absurdity' Is the Fun," *CNN* (March 14, 2017); see also Dana Feldman, "Why ABC's Perfect Summer Escape 'Bachelor in

Paradise' Is Ratings Gold," *Forbes* (August 24, 2018).

56. Michelle Ruiz, "Why Feminists Are Unabashedly Obsessed with *The Bachelor*," *Vogue* (January 10, 2017).

57. In one recent season, after the show had wrapped, Bachelor Arie Luyendyk changed his mind about which woman he preferred. This provoked the explosive ire of the show's fanbase. For a good recap of the incident, see De Elizabeth, "Why Fans of The Bachelor Are Just as Responsible for Becca Kufrin's Heartbreak as Arie," *Allure* (March 6, 2018).

58. Jennifer Gerson Uffalussy, "The slut-shaming on The Bachelorette's 'Men Tell All' episode was a disgrace," *The Guardian* (July 21, 2015).

59. Today the debate is not merely a matter of left progressivism and right conservatism, as it may've been in previous decades, but rather a debate within the Left about whether to abolish the traditional family or instead shore it up. Compare Sophie Lewis, *Full Surrogacy Now*, (New York: Verso, 2019), to Elizabeth Bruenig, "Want millennials to get married and have babies? Change the policies that stop us," *Washington Post* (May 29, 2019).

60. Shulamith Firestone, *Dialectic of Sex* (New York: Farrar, Straus and Giroux, 1970), p. 131.

61. See Bruce Benderson, Interview with Bradford Nordeen, *Lambda Literary* (April 22, 2014).

62. Simone de Beauvoir, *The Second Sex* (New York: First Vintage Books, 1949), p. 439.

63. Juliet Mitchell, *Woman's Estate* (New York: Vintage Books, 1973), p. 153.

64. See Stephanie Convery, "Does bingeing on The Bachelor make me a bad feminist?" *The Guardian* (July 28, 2016).

65. See Kate Julian, "Why Are Young People Having So Little Sex?" *The Atlantic* (December 2018); see further Ashley Fetters and Kaitlyn Tiffany, "The 'Dating Market' Is Getting Worse," *The Atlantic* (February 25, 2020).

66. See Mark Greif, "Octomom and the Market in Babies," *Against Everything* (New York: Pantheon Books, 2016), pp. 56-66.
67. Carol Gilligan and Naomi Snider, *Why Does Patriarchy Persist?* (Cambridge: Polity Press, 2018).

Chapter 7

68. Michael Wolff, *Fire and Fury: Inside the Trump White House* (New York: Henry Holt and Co., 2018). p. 71.
69. Nina Power, *One Dimensional Woman* (Zero Books, 2009), pp. 7-10.
70. Jessa Crispin, *Why I Am Not a Feminist: A Feminist Manifesto* (Brooklyn: Melville House, 2017).
71. Wolfgang Streeck, *Buying Time: The Delayed Crisis of Democratic Capitalism* (New York: Verso, 2017).
72. Nancy Fraser, "Contradictions of Capital and Care," *New Left Review* (vol. 100 July/August 2016).
73. For readers interested in horseshoes, see Tucker Carlson, "Elizabeth Warren encouraged married, two-parent families 16 years ago. She can't do that today," *Fox News* (January 9, 2019).
74. John Kraszewski, *Reality TV* (New York: Routledge, 2017), p. 83.
75. See Eric Dirnbach, "Global Sweatshops, Solidarity and the Bangladesh Breakthrough," *Public Seminar* (January 28, 2016).
76. Cedric Durand, *Fictitious Capital: How Finance is Appropriating Our Future* (New York: Verso, 2018), p. 4.
77. Yann Moulier Boutang, *Cognitive Capitalism* (New York: Polity, 2012), p. 50.
78. Cristina Morini, "The Feminization of Labour in Cognitive Capitalism," *Feminist Review* (vol. 87, 2008).
79. Adam Tooze, *Crashed: How a Decade of Financial Crises Changed the World* (New York: Viking, 2018), p. 25.

Chapter 8

80. Jake Coyle, "Why the success of 'Captain Marvel' is a defeat for trolls," *PBS News Hour* (March 13, 2019).
81. Nancy Fraser, "The End of Progressive Neoliberalism," *Dissent* (January 2, 2017).
82. Jameson, *Postmodernism*, p. 4.
83. Slavoj Žižek, *Like a Thief in Broad Daylight: Power in the Era of Post-Human Capitalism*, (New York: Seven Stories Press, 2019).
84. See Deery, *Reality TV*, p. 7-11.
85. Troy DeVolld, *Reality TV*, p. xv.
86. Jeff Hayden, "How Reality TV Gets Made: an Exclusive Interview with Mark Cronin, Executive Producer of 'Below Deck,'" *Inc.* (September 6, 2016).
87. Robin Young, "Andy Cohen on 'Housewives,' Late-Night Talks and His Disagreement with Gloria Steinem," *WBUR* (January 4, 2017).
88. Firth, Roderick, "Ethical Absolutism and the Ideal Observer," *Philosophy and Phenomenological Research* 12, no. 3 (1952): 317-45.
89. Colby, Georgina. *Bret Easton Ellis: Underwriting the Contemporary* (New York: Palgrave Macmillan, 2011).

Chapter 9

90. Jodi Dean, *Democracy and Other Neoliberal Fantasies* (Durham & London: Duke University Press, 2009).
91. Jameson, *Postmodernism*, p. 38.

Author Biography

Tom Syverson is a writer and editor living in Brooklyn. Over the past few years, he's written regularly on politics and culture for online outlets like Paste Magazine, Quartz, and Splice Today. He can be reached on Twitter: @syvology

CULTURE, SOCIETY & POLITICS

The modern world is at an impasse. Disasters scroll across our smartphone screens and we're invited to like, follow or upvote, but critical thinking is harder and harder to find. Rather than connecting us in common struggle and debate, the internet has sped up and deepened a long-standing process of alienation and atomization. Zer0 Books wants to work against this trend. With critical theory as our jumping off point, we aim to publish books that make our readers uncomfortable. We want to move beyond received opinions.

Zer0 Books is on the left and wants to reinvent the left. We are sick of the injustice, the suffering and the stupidity that defines both our political and cultural world, and we aim to find a new foundation for a new struggle.

If this book has helped you to clarify an idea, solve a problem or extend your knowledge, you may want to check out our online content as well. Look for Zer0 Books: Advancing Conversations in the iTunes directory and for our Zer0 Books YouTube channel.

Popular videos include:

Žižek and the Double Blackmain

The Intellectual Dark Web is a Bad Sign

Can there be an Anti-SJW Left?

Answering Jordan Peterson on Marxism

Follow us on Facebook
at https://www.facebook.com/ZeroBooks and Twitter at https://twitter.com/Zer0Books

Bestsellers from Zer0 Books include:

Give Them An Argument
Logic for the Left
Ben Burgis
Many serious leftists have learned to distrust talk of logic. This is
a serious mistake.
Paperback: 978-1-78904-210-8 ebook: 978-1-78904-211-5

Poor but Sexy
Culture Clashes in Europe East and West
Agata Pyzik
How the East stayed East and the West stayed West.
Paperback: 978-1-78099-394-2 ebook: 978-1-78099-395-9

An Anthropology of Nothing in Particular
Martin Demant Frederiksen
A journey into the social lives of meaninglessness.
Paperback: 978-1-78535-699-5 ebook: 978-1-78535-700-8

Cartographies of the Absolute
Alberto Toscano, Jeff Kinkle
An aesthetics of the economy for the twenty-first century.
Paperback: 978-1-78099-275-4 ebook: 978-1-78279-973-3

Malign Velocities
Accelerationism and Capitalism
Benjamin Noys
Long listed for the Bread and Roses Prize 2015, *Malign Velocities*
argues against the need for speed, tracking acceleration
as the symptom of the ongoing crises of capitalism.
Paperback: 978-1-78279-300-7 ebook: 978-1-78279-299-4

Meat Market
Female Flesh under Capitalism
Laurie Penny
A feminist dissection of women's bodies as the fleshy fulcrum of
capitalist cannibalism, whereby women are both consumers and
consumed.
Paperback: 978-1-84694-521-2 ebook: 978-1-84694-782-7

Babbling Corpse
Vaporwave and the Commodification of Ghosts
Grafton Tanner
Paperback: 978-1-78279-759-3 ebook: 978-1-78279-760-9

New Work New Culture
Work we want and a culture that strengthens us
Frithjoff Bergmann
A serious alternative for mankind and the planet.
Paperback: 978-1-78904-064-7 ebook: 978-1-78904-065-4

Romeo and Juliet in Palestine
Teaching Under Occupation
Tom Sperlinger
Life in the West Bank, the nature of pedagogy and the role of a
university under occupation.
Paperback: 978-1-78279-637-4 ebook: 978-1-78279-636-7

Ghosts of My Life
Writings on Depression, Hauntology and Lost Futures
Mark Fisher
Paperback: 978-1-78099-226-6 ebook: 978-1-78279-624-4

Sweetening the Pill
or How We Got Hooked on Hormonal Birth Control
Holly Grigg-Spall
Has contraception liberated or oppressed women?
Sweetening the Pill breaks the silence on the dark side of hormonal
contraception.
Paperback: 978-1-78099-607-3 ebook: 978-1-78099-608-0

Why Are We The Good Guys?
Reclaiming your Mind from the Delusions of Propaganda
David Cromwell
A provocative challenge to the standard ideology that Western
power is a benevolent force in the world.
Paperback: 978-1-78099-365-2 ebook: 978-1-78099-366-9

The Writing on the Wall
On the Decomposition of Capitalism and its Critics
Anselm Jappe, Alastair Hemmens
A new approach to the meaning of social emancipation.
Paperback: 978-1-78535-581-3 ebook: 978-1-78535-582-0

Enjoying It
Candy Crush and Capitalism
Alfie Bown
A study of enjoyment and of the enjoyment of studying. Bown
asks what enjoyment says about us and what we say about
enjoyment, and why.
Paperback: 978-1-78535-155-6 ebook: 978-1-78535-156-3

Color, Facture, Art and Design
Iona Singh
This materialist definition of fine-art develops guidelines for
architecture, design, cultural-studies and ultimately social
change.
Paperback: 978-1-78099-629-5 ebook: 978-1-78099-630-1

Neglected or Misunderstood
The Radical Feminism of Shulamith Firestone
Victoria Margree
An interrogation of issues surrounding gender, biology,
sexuality, work and technology, and the ways in which our
imaginations continue to be in thrall to ideologies of maternity
and the nuclear family.
Paperback: 978-1-78535-539-4 ebook: 978-1-78535-540-0

How to Dismantle the NHS in 10 Easy Steps (Second Edition)
Youssef El-Gingihy
The story of how your NHS was sold off and why you will have
to buy private health insurance soon. A new expanded second
edition with chapters on junior doctors' strikes and government
blueprints for US-style healthcare.
Paperback: 978-1-78904-178-1 ebook: 978-1-78904-179-8

Digesting Recipes
The Art of Culinary Notation
Susannah Worth
A recipe is an instruction, the imperative tone of the expert, but
this constraint can offer its own kind of potential. A recipe need
not be a domestic trap but might instead offer escape – something
to fantasise about or aspire to.

Paperback: 978-1-78279-860-6 ebook: 978-1-78279-859-0

Most titles are published in paperback and as an ebook.
Paperbacks are available in traditional bookshops. Both print and
ebook formats are available online.
Follow us on Facebook
at https://www.facebook.com/ZeroBooks
and Twitter at https://twitter.com/Zer0Books